You Can Mentor.

ISBN: 978-1-7353469-7-7

A Publication of Tall Pine Books
| tallpinebooks.com

*Printed in the United States of America

You Can Mentor.

HOW TO IMPACT YOUR COMMUNITY, FULFILL THE GREAT COMMISSION, AND BREAK GENERATIONAL ~~CURSES~~.

ZACHARY GARZA

"With great joy and without hesitation I heartily recommend Zachary Garza and the Forerunner Mentoring program which he established in the Dallas area. I have known Zach for years and communicate with him regularly. He's a devout man of God, a devoted husband, and father to his own children as well as surrogate father to many young men. I believe this book needs to be widely circulated and the ministry emulated."

—DON FINTO, PhD.
Pastor emeritus, Belmont Church in Nashville Tennessee
www.donfinto.org

"Zach Garza is that rare man you meet and know instantly you've met the real Zach. He is who he appears to be, which means you can trust what he has to say. Zach has dedicated his life to providing young men with one of the most desperately needed resources in our world today: men who are physically, emotionally, and spiritually present."

—RYAN CASEY WALLER
Therapist and Author of *Depression, Anxiety, and Other Things We Don't Want to Talk About*

"I can wholeheartedly endorse the character, witness, and experience of Zach Garza in the Great Commision call to discipleship. From the day we met to today he's been one of the most intentional to normalize discipleship in our city and our generation."

—GRANT SKELDON
Next Gen Director of Q, Author of *The Passion Generation*

"Many of the problems of our day can be traced back to the lack of a strong, healthy father figure in the home. In a world that is lacking fathers, Zach Garza stands out as an excellent father, a qualified mentor and an inspiring visionary. This book will no doubt be an invaluable resource for those who are willing to engage with the next generations with greater purpose and intentionality."

—PETER K. LOUIS
Author and founder of *Braveheart Ministries*

"Fatherlessness is an epidemic in our culture. Paul said in 1 Corinthians, 'though you have countless guides in Christ, you do not have many fathers'. Zach Garza is a father to the fatherless God has placed His heart inside of Zach to restore sons back to the heart of their Father. If you have met Zach, you have met the heart of a God as a father. He is modeling this for us all in his family, his ministry and his friendship. A generation is being transformed through Zach and his ministry where countless orphaned students will find family and a new definition for Godly love and leadership."

—MICHAEL MILLER
Lead Pastor of *Upperroom Global*
Dallas, Texas

"There is no one I have ever met who thinks more about mentoring than Zach Garza. He doesn't just think about it, though. Zach has put his entire life into leading through mentoring and helping others catch the vision for this essential ministry. Zach is a thinker and a doer and he is whole-heartedly committed to mentoring and mentoring mentors for the sake of the coming kingdom."

—ADAM GRIFFIN
Lead Pastor of *Eastside Church*
author of *Family Discipleship*

"One of the most serious challenges facing the church in North America is that of an undisciplined Gen Z. Zach Garza work seeks to move the norm of passivity in the church into the wondrous adventure of becoming passionate followers of Jesus. His ideas are challenging, thought provoking, and will leave you wanting more —youth ministers, teachers, mentors, and parents grab this resource, NOW!!!"

—RASHAWN COPELAND
Founder of *I'm So Blessed Daily*
author of *Start Where You Are*

"The Father heart of God has captured Zach's heart for a generation of kids who need to know they have not been forgotten, but who are fully loved by God. My family has been blessed to watch the Lord use Zach Garza to help transform a generation of young men right here in our community.

You Can Mentor will encourage and equip YOU to do the same in your community. Let's Go."

—STEVE HARDIN
Campus Pastor, *LakePointe Church-WhiteRock*—Dallas, Texas

"Seldom will you find an individual who is so keenly aware of their own brokenness or inescapable need for healing & restoration as you will in Zach Garza. Zach is one of the most humble, God-fearing men I've ever had the privilege of calling friend. Zach uses his personal life experiences as a means to bless current & future generations of young men who will most certainly be better men & fathers as a result of his work & ministry."

—LUKE WHITMIRE
Christian Service Center Site Director
Cross & Crown Mission—Oklahoma City, OK

"Zach isn't simply an author. He's a practitioner. He actually lives what he preaches. If you want to peek behind the curtain of the messy, hard, complicated - yet beautiful, rewarding and transforming - nature of mentoring, this is your book. Read it, and then join in on the fun."

—KEVIN EAST
President, CEO and Mentor
Mentoring Alliance—Tyler, Texas

"I have known Zach for about 10 years now. He has always been a joy to talk with as its mostly about Jesus, his family or mentoring kids from hard places. He passion shines through when you talk with him and he genuinely a forerunner in the mentoring space. This book is a must read for new and veteran mentors. Thank you Zach for putting what God laid on your heart on paper."

—EDWARD FRANKLIN
President/CEO *Voice of Hope Ministries*—Dallas, Texas

"When I meet young men of God in the coming years in our city who honor one another, sacrifice, trust God, tell the truth and give thanks in all things, I believe that, in part, these will be men influenced by Forerunner Mentoring. Zachary Garza not only leads an effective mentoring ministry growing these values in young men, but he also embodies these values. Nothing speaks louder than that. God has clearly defined Zach's mission to mentor young men and change the trajectory of their lives for the glory of God. I, for one, can't wait to watch his influence change our city."

—JEFF FRITSCHE
Lead Pastor, *White Rock Fellowship*—Dallas, Texas

"Mentoring is part science and part art. Zach Garza and his team have implemented the science of evidence-based mentoring practices along with art of how to connect with kids to establish a unique model for mentoring in Dallas. They have done this all in the context of a ministry that brings the love and truth of our Savior to kids growing up with limited resources and opportunities to enable them to reach their God-given potential."

—PETER VANACORE
MSW, Executive Director
Christian Association of Youth Mentoring

"Zach Garza is the real deal. Zach lives out what many of us just talk about, he embraces the principles and teaching that many of us simply admire. In a world that is taken by words and rhetoric, Zach stands out as a man of action. Zach is exactly the kind of author our generation needs: someone whose words on the page are an extension of their life lived in the mission field. We will all do well to heed the wisdom Zach offers."

—MATT TUGGLE
Executive Minister
Highland Park UMC—Dallas, Texas

"Finding someone who cares about mentoring, youth and the heart of a person as much as Zach does is almost impossible. He has dedicated his life and time to not just the support of others but find away to create opportunities for freedom and growth in the most vulnerable of all of us. Trust me, read this book, apply it to your life and then buy a copy for you friend. We all need this in our life."

—ROCKY GARZA
Truth-Teller | Encourager | Challenger
www.rockygarza.com

"Theodore Roosevelt once described "The Man in the Arena" and my friend Zach could easily fit that description. He is a man "whose face is marred by dust and sweat and blood; who spends himself in a worthy cause." My friend has given his life to the cause of the fatherless. Over the years I've seen Zach dare greatly time and time again. This book is an extension of his life, character and passion. I am pleased to recommend both his book and his life."

—JS BOWER
Pastor, Husband, Father of 5
www.JSBOWER.com

Dedicated to Steve Allen, the best mentor a man could ask for.
If I become half the man you are, I will consider my life a great success.
Here's to raising up 10,000 fathers in the name of Jesus.
The best is yet to come.

Contents

Foreword

I became acquainted with Zach when his life was turning more and more toward Jesus. I did not know the Zach during those earlier years of insecurity, fear, anxiety, rebellion, and rage. I've only known the Zach who has a tender heart, the Zach you want your son to become, Zach the leader, the Zach who dreams about ways to help others—especially helping young men who live with little or no hope.

I was prepared to love this book and I was not disappointed. When I began reading the Tale of Two Kids chapter, I dreaded reading about a kid who had very little, if any, real family life and in great need of a mentor. Yet I knew I would be reading about the kind of young men for whom Zach pours out his life.

I love Zach's testimony. He is proof that in Jesus we can become what we never had. God uses all the past abuses or difficulties we may have experienced at the hands of others for our good and the good of others as we yield to His transforming power. The mistakes we made, the sins we committed, all become springboards for the radical changes God makes in our lives as we grow more and more in the likeness of Jesus.

Alcoholics Anonymous taught us long ago the best people to help others out of an addiction are those who have been freed from that addiction. Overcomers are best prepared to help others overcome. We should therefore not be surprised that Zach is called to mentor young men who are caught in the life circumstances and patterns which controlled Zach's early life.

Because of his own experiences, Zach learned well what I learned when our oldest grandson asked to live with us. Our grandson came from a broken home and was not doing well. The Lord told me I would help my grandson most by complimenting him for what he was doing right rather than concentrating continually on what he was doing wrong. At first, I was not sure I could find anything he was doing right. But I took the challenge and learned to love and affirm him. Yes, thankfully, he is doing well now.

Read this book with an open heart. Walk with Zach into his world and into the lives of these young kids. Ask the Lord to teach you as you read. Are there those you need to forgive? Who have been your mentors? Who are you to mentor? I pray this book will be widely received, widely read, and widely put into practice.

—DON FINTO

Introduction

There was a time in my life when people cringed when they heard my name. As a kid, teachers didn't want me in their classes and other parents warned their children about hanging out with me. When I was in my twenties, I tried to impress my friends by having the biggest muscles, partying the hardest, and dating the most girls. I was heading down the road to nowhere fast and no slowing down in sight.

Then I got my first mentor.

My mentor was the first man in my life who made me feel loved. He took time out of his day to look me in the eye, listen to what I had to say, and tell me that he was proud of me. There is no way I could be the husband, father, and leader I am today without my first mentor. The Lord used that man to change my life and rewrite my narrative.

Now I run a mentoring organization which comes alongside kids who were just like me. Lives are being changed, one mentoring relationship at a time.

Millions of children today are growing up in some kind of traumatic situation like I did. They don't feel loved, cared for, or supported. These kids have experienced a tremendous amount of pain and hurt and have no place or the tools to heal. Turn on the evening news and you may even see a story about one of these kids. They may not have the words to ask for help, but their actions tell a different story. The young man who joined a gang is really looking for a family to accept him. The young woman going from man to man just wants to be loved and for someone to pay attention to her.

Society calls these kids thugs, misfits, gangsters, losers, failures, and punks. Jesus has another name for them: son and daughter. Precious one.

Jesus wants these kids to experience His love and the freedom that comes from a relationship with Him. He wants to comfort them in their pain and heal their hurts. And so often, He wants to use people like you and me to do it.

You may be thinking, "But I'm not qualified. I don't know the first thing about hanging out with those types of kids." I bet that's what the twelve disciples thought when Jesus asked them to join His crew and look at what happened to them. They changed the world and started a movement—but not because of their words, education, or experience. And it wasn't because people thought they were cool or popular or fun. They changed the world because they said yes to what Jesus asked them to do: go and make disciples.

There are kids in your community right now who do not have one caring adult in their corner. I believe God is asking you, "Will you go and be with them? Will you guide My child toward everything I have for them? Will you love them like I love you?" All He needs is your yes. I believe God is calling you, with all your flaws, insecurities, and doubts, to be used to transform a kid's life.

The Lord transformed my life because an ordinary man said yes to building a relationship with me. That relationship turned a generational curse into a generational blessing.

This book will help you answer the Lord's call to love your neighbor and make disciples. He can do the same thing through you.

You can mentor.

CHAPTER ONE

How Mentoring Changed My Life

MY MOTHER WAS born into a legalistic, religious home that valued other people's opinions of them above all else. When my mother got pregnant out of wedlock as a teenager, it was almost too much for her parents. They told her to marry her boyfriend, forced him to get baptized, and pretended like everything was okay. Mom was divorced within three years. After later experiencing multiple miscarriages, and having a baby who passed away one month after he was born, it is no wonder my mom still battles shame, guilt, and depression to this day.

My father was the second oldest of seven children and raised in the infamous Cabrini-Green projects in Chicago, Illinois. At the time, his community—known for its crime, poverty, and racism—was one of the largest public housing complexes in America. No doubt it was a hard place for a second generation Hispanic-American to grow up. My father had to endure multiple forms of abuse from his alcoholic father and other members of his family. He ran away at the age of eighteen with his teenage love and the mother of his new child.

His newfound freedom didn't last long as my father was drafted into the Air Force to serve in the Korean War. His service was cut short when a family friend called to tell him they found his eighteen-month-old son wandering in the street unattended one night. His girlfriend, strung out on drugs, was neglecting his son. My father received permission from the Air Force to rush home to care for his son. Upon his return, he became a policeman and moved to the city of Dallas.

My parents met, both having children from previous marriages and unresolved difficulties from their childhood. They married within six months and had me a few years after. From the very beginning, they both could tell their marriage was a mistake. Abuse, adultery, and fits of rage all made an appearance during their contentious relationship. They were married for fifteen years before getting divorced. Most of those years were difficult, to say the least.

I was thirteen years old when my father left.

I can still picture my father driving off the day my family broke apart. I remember watching him drive away not knowing what to think but feeling that it was a really big deal. As a young teenager, I couldn't articulate and process the pain in my heart. I wasn't mature enough to say, "I'm hurting, angry, and need someone to lead me." Instead, I sank into a dark season which lasted over a decade.

I don't remember a lot from my childhood. My counselor once said I suffer from "repressed memories," which basically means my brain blocked out most of my childhood to protect itself from the traumatic events I endured.

I felt unloved, lost, and afraid. I was terrified to become a man and had no one to guide me on this journey called life. Insecurity, anger, and jealousy were decaying any potential I had.

Because I deeply desired for someone to pay attention to me, I did whatever my friends wanted me to do. I disrespected teachers and authority figures because I didn't trust adults. I was reluctant to share my heart with anyone, even to those who loved me and wanted the best for me. I used drugs and alcohol to numb myself from my feelings and to escape reality. I wanted so badly to be loved that I would give my heart to any girl who showed me the least bit of interest. I was an absolute mess from the age of thirteen to about twenty-two.

When I look at where I was and where I am today, I am convinced the Lord transformed my life through relationships with mentors. These men saw a teenaged kid going through a hard time and stepped in to help. I learned how to fulfill my potential because older men equipped me with tools and confidence to deal with my past. I am who

I am today because of mentoring relationships.

***

Fred was my neighbor. A five feet, ten inches southern Baptist architect who had salt and pepper hair and three girls of his own. I remember him picking me up one night a few weeks after my parents split to take me out to eat and go see a movie. Fred saw a hurting kid and decided to do something about it. I don't remember much about my childhood, but I can tell you everything about that one night. In a season of hurt and darkness, that evening with Fred was a sliver of light. Every time I see a Razoo's restaurant or eat fried pickles, I think of Fred and his investment in my life.

God worked through Jason, the youth group intern. I can't remember Jason's last name, but I do remember him taking me to Albuquerque, New Mexico on a church mission trip. I can still remember where I was sitting when he told me how excited he was to get back to his new wife and how awesome marriage was.

A few weeks later, Jason called and asked me to play basketball with him at the local recreation center. He knew I loved hoops. He picked me up in the stark white, fifteen-passenger church van. We listened to rap music on the way to the gym, which I'm pretty sure was against church policy. I don't think I've ever played basketball as hard as I did that day. I wanted to impress Jason with all of my skills. He left a month later but wrote me a letter encouraging me to follow Jesus and be a leader. Over twenty years later, I still have the letter.

Mentors like Fred and Jason kept me from going too far down a bad path. Although I was up to no good when these mentors came into my life, every interaction with them kept me closer to the good side. They were the ones who set the stage for the next set of mentors who impacted me.

***

During my freshman year of college, I continued to rebel, act out, and get my needs met in all the wrong places. And I needed a job. That's when I found out about summer camps and the opportunity to get paid while hanging out with kids and entertaining them throughout the summer.

I interviewed with a short, bald, older gentleman named Bob. He hired me to work with him that summer. I couldn't have been more excited to work with kids and to finally have a job.

I liked Bob instantly because he loved me for me. He didn't judge me, and my big personality wasn't too much for him. My reputation on campus as a party boy preceded me, but he took a shot on me. Bob would later tell me, "We hired fifty camp counselors that year. Forty-seven of those counselors were good for camp. But for three of those counselors, camp was good for them. You were one of the three."

I spent a lot of time around Bob during my college years. Whether I was stopping by his office in the middle of the day to talk about the New York Yankees or going to his parent's house for a camp staff dinner, Bob made me feel like I mattered—and I hadn't felt that from a man in a several years. On the surface, it seemed like I just enjoyed being around Bob, but subconsciously I was spending time with him because he was meeting my needs for affirmation and acceptance in a healthy way. He provided me with a Christ-centered, positive example as I entered manhood. Bob did that for me over the next three summers as I continued to work for him.

One evening, Bob invited me to a Bible study. Bob knew I was angry with God for my parent's divorce. I thought God was just like all the old, legalistic, crotchety old men who went to my childhood church. Bob invited me anyways. Normally, I would never have gone to a Bible study. But I had so much respect for Bob, I would do whatever he asked me to do.

I walked in the room fully expecting not to pay attention. But during the study, Bob started to talk about fathers. At this point in my life, any talk of fathers caused me to become overwhelmed with anger.

I remember balling up my fists when Bob said, "God put fathers here on earth to represent Him. In a perfect world, your father is like God. He's kind, a protector, and a provider. It's easy to see God as a good father if you have a good father here on earth. But for some of you, your father might be the opposite of God. And if that's the case, I want to share with you that God still loves you and is still your father."

The Holy Spirit began to soften my calloused heart when I heard those words. I hadn't cried since my father left when I was thirteen, and all of those pent-up emotions were now coming out. Embarrassed, I ran out of the room and went to be by myself.

Bob was right behind me. Once he found me, he grabbed me by the back of the neck and pulled me into his chest for a hug. As he held me, Bob spoke truth to me, phrases like, "I love you" and "I'm proud of you." Then he said one phrase I'll never forget: "Zach, you have to deal with your past because it is killing your future."

I wish I could say I hopped on the straight and narrow path from that day forward. But it took me almost six more years to fully start walking in freedom. The Lord changed my life that night and He used my relationship with Bob to do it. Through my relationship with Bob, the Lord broke off the generational curses that plagued me since childhood. God used my relationship with Bob to take me off the path of darkness and to put me on a new path of light.

***

Over the following years, other mentors entered my life to help me heal from the traumas of my childhood.

God introduced me to Joel and Mandy. Joel showed me you could be cool and love Jesus at the same time. Through chicken tetrazzini and sweet tea, Mandy created a safe and loving environment for me to truly be myself.

The Lord had me cross paths with Randy, an older guy at church, who called me out for acting selfish in dating relationships. He taught me how to pursue a woman in a Godly way.

Paul and Kelly were the parents of a girl I dated. Paul invited me to sit at his table and I watched him lead as a husband and father. Being around Kelly is where I learned how to ask questions, talk less, and listen more. When I told Paul I had some things from my past I needed to deal with, he introduced me to his friend, Alex.

Alex gently highlighted my pride by pointing out my reluctance to open up and trust people. He also helped me identify how my anger and bitterness, which came from the unforgiveness I had toward my father, was negatively impacting my life.

My friend John taught me how to be disciplined, wake up early, and spend time with God. John and his wife, Michelle, showed me what a healthy marriage looked like.

It was during this season of transformation I decided to make Jesus my Lord and Savior. For the first time ever, I decided to chase after the Lord. Instead of running to the bar or to women to get my needs met, I chose to run to Jesus.

My choice to follow Jesus brought me to a summer discipleship training school in Nashville, Tennessee. A teacher by trade, I was fortunate to have summers off and I wanted to use that time to grow closer to Jesus. At this program, I met the most important man in my life.

I was twenty-five-years old the first time I met Steve Allen. As a new believer and unfamiliar in my relationship with Jesus, it was hard for me to be in a discipleship program surrounded by mature believers. I felt like I wasn't good enough. Steve told me otherwise. He was a source of comfort for me as I was doubting my newfound faith.

Over the next few weeks, Steve spoke into my life in a gentle yet powerful way. Steve never gave advice, but only asked questions. Steve's pointed questions, mixed in with the guidance of the Holy Spirit and my burning desire to become more like Jesus, created the perfect storm for a life transformation. God feeds the hungry and I was definitely hungry for more of the only thing that had proven to satisfy my desires.

Steve asked questions like, "What is God's vision for your life?" and "What is keeping you from meeting your father to forgive him face-to-face?" The Lord used those questions to pierce my heart and help me realized I had no plan for my life and I was terrified to look my father in the eyes and say, "I forgive you." Over the next few months, Steve helped me overcome both.

In the following years, Steve helped me become a godly husband and lead my family with intentionality and servant leadership. He supported me as I stepped away from my teaching and coaching career to launch a mentoring nonprofit organization. He cried with me as my wife and I experienced multiple miscarriages, and he celebrated with me and my wife at the births of our children. When I had a personal crisis that almost cost me my ministry, Steve was the one who consistently prayed with me and pointed me back to Jesus.

To this day, I still talk to Steve every week. He is my guide. He gives me someone to emulate and challenges me to grow as a man of God. I named my second-born son Stephen to honor him. If my son becomes half the man Steve Allen is, I will consider that a major success.

God really did have a plan for my life, a plan for me to prosper (Jeremiah 29:11). The enemy wanted to use my childhood and generational sins to destroy me. But what the enemy uses for evil, God can use for good. I had no hope and no future, but the Lord provided both for me. He did all those things through mentors. Godly men stepped up to the challenge, whether intentionally or unintentionally, and built a relationship with a cocky kid who had anger issues.

The Lord works in mysterious ways and it is only in hindsight that I can appreciate His work. I thought Fred and I were just going to a movie, but instead, the Lord was keeping me on the right path. Working at a summer camp was just a job to me, but the Lord was using Bob to change my heart. I thought the summer discipleship program would be fun, but it was there the Lord led me to Steve. And nothing has been the same since.

But tragically, my story is the exception. Most kids from tough backgrounds don't get the second chance my mentors provided for me. Without the love, attention, and guidance from an adult who cares about them, most kids never recover from the pain and experiences of their childhood.

Almost half the nation's children have experienced trauma.[1] According to the National Child Traumatic Stress Initiative in 2015, more than two thirds of children report at least one traumatic event by age sixteen.[2] Fathers.com reports over twenty million children are growing up in a home without their father present.[3] In 2013, The Guardian stated thirteen million kids are living in poverty.[4] Unless someone intervenes and helps our children overcome these obstacles, they may never have a chance to maximize their potential.

God created us to be in relationship with Him and others. Satan wants to destroy anything that gives anyone life to the fullest, especially the next generation. But God has a plan. God wants us to love Him and love others. He wants to express His love, kindness, and grace through us.

The Lord calls us to make disciples—to transform the life of one or more of His beloved children. His desire is to express His heart for youth through your loving actions. He wants to remove aloneness through relationship and is looking for someone to volunteer. He is looking for someone just like you.

You can be a mentor.

CHAPTER TWO

A Tale of Two Kids

EIGHT-YEAR-OLD John wakes up in his own room, in his own bed, to the sound of his mother singing, "Wake up, you sleepy head. Get up, get out of bed..."

As he stumbles into the kitchen, John sees that Mom has already made him his usual hearty breakfast of eggs, bacon, a glass of milk, and a banana. While he eats, John answers his mom's questions about the upcoming school day.

After breakfast, John scurries up the stairs to get ready for school.

John picks his favorite shirt to wear. It reads, "Future Class President of State University." John's grandfather, a proud State Alum, gave him the shirt for his birthday last year. The note attached read: "If you make good grades and stay out of trouble, I'll do anything I can to help you graduate State, just like your father and I did. Love you kid, Grandpa."

Full from his healthy breakfast and looking good, John packs his backpack with his school supplies and hops into his mother's car. Time to go to school.

As John enters the school building, he sees his best friend, Matthew.

"You ready for that test today?" Matthew falls into step next to

John.

"Mom made me study for like three hours last night," says John.

John and Matthew attend a good school full of good kids. The students take their education seriously because their parents took their education seriously. As John gets to class, he is welcomed by Ms. Potter, the nicest and prettiest teacher he's ever had.

Class begins.

After a few hours, the bell rings for lunch. John races to the cafeteria to get a seat by Matthew. John opens his sack lunch to find a note: "I believe in you, Champ. Make it a great day! Dad."

John finishes up the day without any issues. The school bell ringing, John and Matthew race outside to get picked up by Matthew's mother.

At home, John's mom greets him. "How was school today, buddy? You ready to tackle your homework?"

John and his mother start working on the day's homework after a quick trip to the store to grab poster board, markers, and a glue stick for his science project.

About the time John starts on his project, his father arrives from work.

"Daaaaaaa-d's home!" John's dad yells in a funny voice as he walks in the back door.

Dad gives Mom a big hug and an even bigger kiss. John rolls his eyes and acts grossed out, but really, he loves watching his dad love on his mom.

During dinner, John's dad takes the lead. "Ok family, highs and lows. Mom, you go first."

They take turns sharing about their day. They do this almost every night.

"May I be excused?" John says as he chows down the last bite of his meatloaf.

"Sure, son," his dad says. "Remember, we got basketball practice in thirty minutes."

"Oh man, I forgot!" John says. "Monday night. Basketball practice!"

John rushes to get ready for practice then meets his father at the car. Off to practice they go.

On their way home from the gym, John and his father stop to get a milkshake.

"So, you like any girls? And what's new with your friends?" John's dad asks as they sit down to drink their milkshakes.

Back home, John showers and gets ready for bed. His mom reminds him to pack his book bag and science project. She gives him a kiss as he gets into bed. He turns off the light thinking how excited he is for school tomorrow. He's excited to see Mrs. Potter, Matthew, and show off his science project to his peers.

Before he drifts off to sleep, John's dad comes in.

"I really enjoyed spending time with you today. You're the man! Love you. Proud of you." John's dad gives him a kiss on the check. "Sweet dreams, my son."

***

"Aww, man! I'm gonna miss my bus! Stupid, piece of junk alarm clock." Eight-year-old Mike tries his hardest to be as fast and quiet as possible getting dressed. His mom is sound asleep, and he knows her working two jobs as a single mom is no joke.

Mike runs down the stairs of the apartment complex and sees police cars in the parking lot. "Must be here because of the gunshots I heard last night," he mutters.

Mike doesn't care much for his new school. Life has been hard since he had to move schools and leave his old community. But he's moved with his mom every two years for as long as he can remember.

Mike gets to school cold, hungry, and late. He has a choice: does he get a tardy so he can stop by the cafeteria to grab some breakfast, or go straight to class hungry? He chooses food.

He hears the tardy bell as he gets in line. "Man, breakfast pizza again? This stuff is nasty." Finished with his stale pizza and chocolate milk, Mike walks to class.

"Well, good to see you today, Michael!" says Ms. Smith in a sarcastic tone. "You're late. That's detention."

Mike stares at the ground. He really doesn't like Ms. Smith.

"And no backpack again?" she continues.

Everyone knows Ms. Smith doesn't like her job since she got transferred to this underperforming campus. Her go-to line is, "What's wrong with you kids? Why can't you act right?"

After class, Ms. Smith reminds Mike about his lunch detention. He goes to the cafeteria to grab his lunch of fries, pizza, and fruit punch. "Today sucks," he says as he carries his lunch to Ms. Smith's room.

Mike is startled by a sudden announcement over the loudspeaker: "Students, please walk down to the auditorium for our assembly."

"Yes!" Mike says to himself, excited to leave Ms. Smith's class.

Mike takes a seat in the auditorium. "Welcome to College and Career Week, my scholars!" says the principal. The only thing Mike knows about college is that his mom tried to take some night classes but quit to work another job to make ends meet. Mike takes a nap.

Brrrrrring!

Mike is awoken by the sound of the bell.

"School's out! Thank God." Mike says.

Mike decides to walk home. It's not like he has anything to do or anyone waiting for him at home.

Minding his own business, he sees a bunch of older teenagers smoking weed up ahead. Mike walks faster, remembering the time last year when his cousin was robbed because of his headphones. As the teenagers stare Mike down, he turns right and takes the long way home.

Mike makes it to his apartment and finds a note from his mom. "Love you, son. I hope you had a good day at school. Don't go play outside. It's too dangerous. I'll be home late."

Mike goes to do his homework, but remembers his backpack is still in his mom's car. "Dang, Ms. Smith is going to kill me tomorrow."

Mike is alone. He doesn't have anything else to do, or anyone to talk to, and it's only 5:00.

"Maybe I'll watch TV for a few minutes." He plops down on the couch with a bag of chips and a soda as he watches LeBron highlight videos. "Maybe one day I can be like LeBron," Mike mumbles as he starts to doze off.

When Mike's mom comes home after midnight, she sees her baby asleep on the couch with the TV on. She runs her fingers through his hair and starts to cry. "This isn't the life I want to give my boy," she says to herself. "He deserves better than this."

The Issue

Tens of millions of kids just like Mike are growing up in our country today, kids who have been dealt a tough hand in life. These kids have experienced more obstacles in their childhood than most people do in their entire lives. These negative experiences create an uphill battle for the rest of their lives and hinder them from fulfilling their God-given potential.

These experiences and hindrances are traumas that severely impact the child's life. The crazy thing about trauma is this: not all overwhelming or life-threatening experiences are considered traumatic. Children interpret their experiences differently. A similar life experience that is traumatic for one child might not be for another. Every situation is different, and every child is different, so there is no telling how a trauma (or multiple traumas) will impact a specific child.

I've known a child who experienced multiple severe traumas in his life and overcome them without much adversity. I've also seen one traumatic situation stunt a child's maturity and keep him from becoming all he can be. There is no "one size fits all" when it comes to trauma.

Being poor is going to make life more difficult for a child—even more so if they don't have a father around and don't know where the next meal is coming from. Moving every couple of years, which causes a child to potentially change schools and friend groups, affects their sense of stability and security.

Imagine the toll experiencing physical, sexual, or emotional abuse can have on an eight-year-old child. Think about how neglect, whether intentional by a hurtful adult or unintentional by an overworked parent, can affect a child. Consider how living in a dangerous environment, one where you are constantly worried about gunshots, robberies, or violence can mess with a kid's mind. Think about what kind of impact the loss of a loved one, due to drug or alcohol abuse or domestic violence, can have on a child's wellbeing. And we haven't even started to discuss incarceration, racism, and bullying.

Any of one of the issues above would negatively impact the healthiest of adults. Pile on two or three or four of these traumas and most children don't stand a chance to have a healthy, resilient life. These are the obstacles that face thousands of children in your community day after day.

As stated in an article titled "Trauma" on *Psychology Today*'s website, sufferers of trauma may develop emotional disturbances such as extreme anxiety, anger, sadness, stress, survivor's guilt, or Post Traumatic Stress Disorder (PTSD). Children who have experienced traumas perform worse academically, have poor health, and exhibit behavioral issues. These children are not as likely to graduate high school as seventy-one percent of high school dropouts are from fatherless homes, get a job which provides a livable wage, or even have a job altogether. Chances of these children growing up to experience homelessness, incarceration, and substance abuse skyrocket along with the chances of teen pregnancy and emotional and psychological issues.[5]

Let's go down this rabbit trail a little further. Let's say you have one hundred kids who have experienced trauma in your community and half those kids end up doing poorly in school, having anger or self-esteem issues, and lack purpose and vision. There is a high likelihood that, unless someone intervenes, these fifty kids will be engaging with and influencing your community in some way—and typically, not in a positive way. While these kids carry the trauma they endure, they are attending neighborhood schools. Statistics show that children from father-absent homes are four times more likely to live in poverty. Perhaps they depend on governmental financial assistance. The chances of them gaining employment go down and the chances of them committing a crime go up. Maybe they will have children of their own who will also grow up in a dysfunctional home, repeating the cycle. I'm not saying this will definitely happen for each child, but the chances are high and it is easy to see how it can happen.

All these issues have an impact on our communities, our economy, and our schools. No one benefits when a child experiences trauma and it causes them to act in a negative way. When one child suffers, the entire village suffers.

So, what is our response?

I've heard a number of different solutions, from encouraging these kids and teenagers to work harder, to emphasizing education, to getting a job. But working harder doesn't help a child heal from the wounds of perpetual hunger and fear of being evicted. Education can't eliminate the anger and self-confidence which stems from the wounds that occurred when his father left. Being successful at a summer or part-time job is hard when you have trust and submission issues with authority and no idea how to network or respond to constructive feedback.

Some people say it has to do with information: reading books, podcasts, sermons, and memorizing Bible verses. But books won't give you a long hug after you find out that your best friend just died. Podcasts can't encourage you when you start to doubt yourself and are contemplating suicide. Sermons are good, but even the most compelling sermon can't sit you down, look you in the eyes, and say "I love you no matter what and I'm proud of you" when you find out you're pregnant out of wedlock. Preaching "God has a plan" and "trust in God" isn't the most comforting thing to hear when the only thing you want is to see your father, but he's stuck in prison for the next twenty-five years.

The poor, the marginalized, the fatherless, the brokenhearted, the hungry—those who have experienced injustice, the oppressed—these are the kids we are talking about. And these are exactly the people who God called us to serve.

The Solution

The solution for all these issues is found only in relationship.

We were made for relationships. It doesn't matter race, age, socioeconomic status, gender, or language—every single person needs human interaction. We were made to be connected to each other. God made us like this on purpose and for our good.

At the start of humanity, in the Garden of Eden, God provided everything we needed. He gave us morning so we could work and evening so we could rest. He gave us land to cultivate and the seas to explore. He gave us vegetation and fruit, crops and trees that would feed us. He gave us animals of all shapes and sizes to join us on the earth. He gave us the sun, moon, and the stars. Lastly, He gave humans dominion over it all. And it was good.

But then something happened. God says a phrase which forever changed the world: "It is not good for man to be alone" (Genesis 2:18). And He created someone for Adam. And that was the perfect life. Adam had Eve. Eve had Adam. There was relationship with each other and relationship with God. Even in the Garden of Eden, where there was no sin and all was perfect, God's plan was always about re-lationships.

In a perfect world, when relationships are going well, the result is always fruit. That is how it's supposed to go. That is how God set up the world. God wants you in a loving, supportive family. He wants you in His spiritual family. He wants to let you know you are His child, He is a good father, and He would do anything to be with you.

He put biological families here on earth to be a little taste of what His family in heaven is like.

The enemy knows if he can destroy the family, then he can shake the foundation of our very being. I'm sure all of us are close to some-one who has been impacted by family drama, estranged relationships, adultery, divorce, or domestic violence. The health of your family in-fluences everything you do and every relationship you have. It even shapes the way you see God.

The ruining of familial relationships is at the core of Satan's plan to destroy humanity. The enemy knows if he can negatively impact a child early on, then he doesn't have to worry about that person in the future. The enemy isolates and then he attacks.

Picture Mike's mother. Imagine her life as a single mother. May-be she is a refugee. Maybe she's a minority. Maybe she has unhealed trauma from her childhood. Whatever the case, she is on her own and she's doing the best she can. When she is at her weakest, the lies start coming:

- "Why aren't you doing more?"
- "This is all your fault."
- "Your kid's life would be better if only you were better."

For Mike, the lies sound a little different:

- "To be a real man, you must fight."
- "Don't worry about school. It's not important."
- "Don't show your emotions. That's weakness. Don't you dare show the true you. You can be angry though. That's not weak."

The enemy lies. He lied in the Garden of Eden and he lies to us today.

While we cannot control the fact that there are single parents and while we cannot protect every child from danger or trauma, we can control if they are alone or not. We can show up on a consistent basis and love them just as they are.

If the young men and young women growing up isolated and without positive role models are anything like me, they are thinking:

- "Who will love me?"
- "Who will teach me how to be successful in life?"
- "Who will show me how to handle life when it doesn't go my way?"

Questions pop up for the single parent as well:

- "Who will teach my child the things I can't teach them?"
- "Who is going to help me take care of my child after school while I work to make ends meet?"
- "Who is going to help me when I am tired, alone, and scared about the future?"

All the while, God is looking down from heaven saying:

- "Who will look after the fatherless and the widow and set the lonely in family?"
- "Who will set the oppressed free and loosen the chains of injustice?"
- "Who will give love and serve those who are the least of these?"

I believe the answer to those questions is you. You can mentor.

CHAPTER THREE

Obstacles in Mentoring

I BEGAN TO mentor Chris in the middle of his seventh-grade year. He was a great kid with an awesome smile. We bonded over football and I had the joy of coaching him during his eighth-grade year. He was an incredible athlete and a true leader among his peers. He looked every bit the part of the tough guy athlete on the outside, but he was sweet and tenderhearted inside.

One day, my wife and I received a call from Chris asking if we could come to his apartment. We drove to his complex not knowing what to expect.

Chris's mother explained she was moving to Detroit to be with a guy she was dating. Chris made it clear he didn't want to leave Dallas as he was finally making good grades, had new friends, and excelling in sports. Seemingly out of nowhere, Chris's mom asked my wife and I if Chris could live with us.

We were shocked.

My wife and I had been married only three months. I was thirty and she was twenty-five. We prayed about it, consulted our community, and decided this is what the Lord had for us.

Chris moved in with us the summer before his freshman year of high school. The first year Chris lived with us was a dream. Chris excelled in school and sports. He made the National Junior Honor's Society and was called up to play varsity football for their playoff game. He had good friends and was making great decisions. Everyone loved Chris and my wife and I really enjoyed having him around the house.

In the middle of the second year, things started to change. We thought maybe it was normal teenage angst, or perhaps the pressures of his sophomore year were getting the best of him. Either way, Chris started lying to us. He stopped trying in school and he snuck out of our house to visit his girlfriend.

Never one to share his emotions, Chris became even more closed off to me. He opened up a little to my wife, but he had constructed what seemed like a ten-foot wall between him and me. I wondered if he even liked me or if we made the right decision by inviting him into our house. Our living environment was filled with tension instead of ease and division instead of peace. It was the darkest season I experienced both as a man and a mentor.

Chris's junior year was a flat-out nightmare. A few moments that stick out to me include Chris exploding in anger at me during a walk around the lake and the two of us yelling at each other in my living room. I remember he took the car my wife and I purchased for him and said he was going to visit his brother in Arkansas. He never showed up at his brother's and disappeared for a week. We found him later because a sheriff pulled him over at 4 a.m. somewhere in East Texas.

Chris snuck out of our house every chance he got and wouldn't answer our phone calls or texts. He was making poor grades, getting in trouble at school, and not taking athletics seriously. He continued to close himself off and we couldn't believe a thing he told us. My wife and I had no idea what to do as we continued to try to invest in Chris's life.

Finally, after giving Chris multiple chances to correct his behavior, my wife and I made the decision to ask Chris to leave our house in the beginning of his senior year. We thought this move might scare him straight, but instead, he was happy to be out on his own. He moved in with a friend and could finally do as he pleased.

A few months later, we got a call telling us Chris had been arrested for a felony and was in police custody. My wife and I were heartbroken and devastated. This wasn't how it was supposed to go. Chris was supposed to come live with us and reach his full potential. I was envisioning college scholarships and campus visits. Now we were visiting him in jail.

How could this happen to me, a self-proclaimed mentoring expert, after investing so much time and energy into Chris? This is the result?

So, what happened?

I believe two major things went wrong in my relationship with Chris. The first thing was my actions showed I valued results over relationship. I wish I would have focused more on his heart than his sports and grades. Secondly, I didn't pay enough attention to his past and the negative experiences he had endured as a child.

***

If we believe it is truly not good for man to be alone and our role as mentors is to build relationships which lead to transformation, then the enemy is going to do everything he can to keep that from happening. He will lie to you, knowing that if he can discourage you, and make you feel like you are not progressing, the chances of you quitting the relationship skyrocket. I almost quit on Chris but thank the Lord my wife and I stuck it out with him. Now he is a father of two and an outstanding young man. We would have missed God redeeming his story if we had quit out of our discouragement.

Trauma from our childhood impacts our lives more than we know. The difficulties and negative experiences in life create obstacles which can discourage even the most equipped of mentors.

Here are a few obstacles which can keep mentors from building relationships with their mentees. While reading these, remember:

- These young people have hurts that are unrealized, unidentified, and unprocessed.
- Depending on personality, two kids can experience the same situation and handle it in two totally different ways.
- Sometimes, these obstacles can actually be a protection mechanism.
- Some of these run together. Fear can cause anger, and insecurity is a form of fear.

Fear

Fear is the foundational obstacle that keeps mentors from investing in the life of their mentee. The only thing Chris wanted in his life was to be loved. He was looking for love first from his family, but when they weren't able to give it to him, he turned to romantic relationships. He just wanted love but was looking for it in all the wrong places.

Why would he try to get his needs met through teenage girls when he had a safe, loving home with my wife and me? We did everything we could to show him acceptance and love—from taking him to college football games to buying him the nicest clothes, showing we valued him and wanted to be with him. We opened our home and gave him access to all we had. But he rejected it. Doesn't make much sense, but fear has a way of doing that to even the strongest of people.

Fear is the most prominent obstacle which prohibits intimate connection between a mentee and mentor. It can force itself into every conversation with and every situation our mentees have. Fear is constantly focused on the negative and it will keep a person from fulfilling their full potential. To make matters worse, the lies of the enemy are gasoline on the fear fire.

The kid who plays video games all day in his room by himself? Perhaps he has a fear of getting out and trying new things. What about the boy who won't try out for a sports team or ask a girl out? Fear can be a major player in that as well. During my junior year of high school, I quit the basketball team, an unusual move for someone who is six feet, eight inches and athletic. I also didn't ask out a girl in high school out of fear of being rejected. I'm not saying I'm the best-looking guy in the world, but I'm sure someone would have gone out with me. I never tried because I was terrified. Fear keeps a kid from taking risks or trying new things. Fear says, "Don't do that. Remember what happened last time you tried something different: you got hurt. You don't want to get hurt again, do you?"

I have a three-year-old son who is as wild as they come. He's always jumping off something or tearing through the house at full speed. The other day, I heard a loud crash come from my son's room followed by a high-pitched scream. I ran into my son's room to find he had jumped off the top bunk of his bed and landed on some toys. He had scraped his knee and it needed to be washed and bandaged quickly. But my son was so scared the pain would get worse if we touched it. We sat there for forty-five minutes, assuring him we were safe and only wanted to help. His fear kept him from receiving what he needed to heal.

Some of our mentees live in this same defense mode. Fear is a vicious cycle. The hearts of our mentees scream, "More than anything, I want to be loved and cared for. But I have so much fear of being hurt, I do things to keep myself from receiving the very love and care I want." They want love, but their actions make them hard to love. It isn't pretty.

For the kids we mentor, I promise you, their hearts want to open up and trust. They want to be guided by you. Their desire is to be loved in a safe and secure environment. But because their past is holding them hostage, they just don't know how to let go of fear.

Insecurity

Hurricane Katrina was one of the worst hurricanes in the history of the United States. Over a thousand people lost their lives and it caused over one hundred billion dollars' worth of damage to the state of Louisiana.

One of the fallouts of Katrina was the displacement of hundreds of thousands of families, many from the most underserved communities near New Orleans. Because of this, the junior high school where I was teaching experienced an influx of new students, specifically from the notorious ninth ward of New Orleans.

Over the next few months, I witnessed at least twenty fights between the kids from New Orleans and our students from Northeast Dallas. There seemed to be at least a fight a week with the same script: two kids trying to act tough to either fit in or impress their friends.

I've taught over a thousand kids in my life and seen a lot of fights. I can count on one hand the number of kids who actually enjoy fighting. The others were just trying to prove something to their friends. Peer pressure is hard to resist, especially in junior high school among insecure students. Chasing after security acceptance offers can cause kids to make decisions that will negatively impact them for the rest of their life.

Because of the hurt our kids have experienced, insecurity runs rampant. This can look like being the tough guy or sexy girl, by pretending everything is okay, or by being overly confident. Insecurity causes a person to do whatever they can to let you know they don't need you or your help. This extreme self-focus is a protection mechanism which keeps potential threats of harm, and most people, at bay.

The inability to be vulnerable is another sign of insecurity. This is the reason an obviously upset kid will answer, "Nothing!" when asked what is wrong. Their insecurity and the fear of being truly known causes them to build a wall between anyone who is trying to get to know them on a deep level. This wall is built on a foundation of "you can trust no one" and consists of one-word answers and resistance to letting you into their life. This also causes difficulties with authority because they don't trust others to care for or lead them well.

Insecure kids don't ask for help because it is a confession of something being wrong, something they can't handle on their own. There is no room for feedback. Even though feedback can be meant to show where he or she needs help or can grow, it can come across as pointing out their wrongs when they've been trying to do their best on their own. If they do show they need help or something is wrong, they are afraid you might leave when you see their flaws. If they don't let you get close, you won't get to know the real them and they will never get to know the real you. If they don't know the real you, they can't reject you.

Anger

I was in my early twenties and my girlfriend and I were going to a concert with her brother and his girlfriend. It was going to be a great night as I had been wanting to see this band in concert for as long as I could remember. As the concert started, the two guys sitting behind us started talking a little bit. Nothing major, but it was definitely distracting. I had paid good money for these seats and this was my favorite band. I turned around, smiled, and politely asked the guys to be quiet. They gave me some sarcastic comment and laughed.

No more Mr. Nice Guy. I jumped over my seat, grabbed the guy by the collar, and screamed profanities in his face. My girlfriend and her brother weren't impressed with my immature reaction. The night didn't turn out how I planned. Anger will do that.

What happened that night is something I call a $500 reaction to a $0.05 problem. The problem I faced was small. It didn't necessitate the major reaction I gave it. But that's what happens when you have trauma and negative emotions you haven't dealt with. You can push all your emotions as far down as you can, but they will still show their ugly face in some unexpected way.

I've seen kids absolutely lose it over the smallest of things. I've witnessed a kid throw a desk across the room because I changed his seat on the seating chart. I've seen two kids get into a fight over a candy bar. More times than not, the issue our kids are facing is not the root of their anger. Perhaps they're mad about being poor or their brother is in prison. Maybe they feel life isn't fair and no one loves them. I've heard the phrase, "I'm just so angry and I don't know why" so many times.

Regardless of the reason, anger is a common emotion that rears its head during some mentoring relationships. No one likes being around someone who is angry. It makes everything more complicated and stressful. Anger in the heart of a mentee can discourage even the best of mentors. Remember the story of Chris and I yelling at each other by the lake? I doubted myself as a mentor for weeks. It is easy to take it personal and believe you were the one who caused this negative emotion.

Remember, the anger keeping us from getting to know our mentee is not our fault. What an opportunity to love our mentee in the middle of his anger, to help him identify it, and process it in a healthy way.

Apathy

Not all kids get angry. The opposite of the angry kid is the apathetic kid. It's not as obvious as anger, but it is just as destructive.

Our patio is connected to the back of our house. Nothing special, just four posts and a roof. My wife and I love to sit back there and watch our kiddos play in the backyard. One day, it was raining, and I noticed a small leak coming from a section of the roof. Not being the least bit handy, I ignored the leak hoping it would go away. This is not the smartest move I have made.

The years passed and the leak got bigger. The leak totally ruined the roof of our patio and the water decayed two of our four main posts.

I finally had a guy out to look at the damage.

"Mister," he said, "if you would have called me three years ago, this would have cost you fifty dollars. Now I have to replace the whole thing. It'll be around five thousand dollars."

On the outside, it seemed like I just didn't care about the leak, but that's not the case. I knew about the leak and thought about it every time it rained. The problem was I had no idea how to fix the problem and I was too scared to face the idea of fixing the leak. I was paralyzed with ignorance and too embarrassed to admit my shortcomings. My inability to know what to do in the situation caused me to become apathetic.

There is nothing more frustrating than a child who seems like they don't care and there is nothing you can do to change it. Unlike anger, apathy is being void of any emotion. It was Chris when we told him he was moving out. He didn't care one bit, or so it looked on the outside.

Failing school? Doesn't matter. Getting evicted? Just another day. Dad goes to prison? Not a big deal. We call this a $0.05 reaction to a $500 problem. It's easy to believe the kid just doesn't care, but I've found that not to be true. The main issue is they don't know how to handle the problem, so they just don't even try.

Or perhaps these kids feel their actions are never good enough. These kids have the mindset that whatever they do, it won't be enough, so they don't try. You might see this if the child has a parent so stricken with fear that they fixate on every little thing their child needs to improve. If their kid is doing one hundred things right and one thing wrong, the child will get an earful about how they need to fix that one. This is the parent who wants to know why their kid scored only 42 points instead of 50 points. No matter how well the child does, the parent will not accept him or her, so the child gives up.

Inability to Receive

Any good mentor wants to help fill up their mentee's love tank, give him or her all the wisdom they have, and help their mentee succeed in life. Mentors start the relationship so excited to share all their expertise and life experience. But what happens when the mentee doesn't receive what you give them? What if they don't care about your math shortcuts or the hug you try to give them?

I never felt loved as a child. Although my mom did the best she could raising me amid difficult circumstances, I often felt alone and unlovable. I'm positive many people loved me during my childhood, but I never *felt* loved. There's a difference between knowing and feeling. And not feeling loved or lovable is a big problem that has caused chaos in my life. The issue has shown up in my marriage and in my adult life. For the longest time, I didn't know how to receive love from my wife. I would squirm when she said nice things about me, and I had a real hard time with intimacy. I couldn't receive her love and this issue stems from my childhood.

I couldn't receive love because I didn't feel worthy. I didn't feel like I deserved it. Receiving unconditional love I hadn't earned was foreign to me. As a child, I could receive praise if I felt like I earned it. Some kids learn the only time the teacher likes them is when they behave well, or the coach only talks to them when they are helping the team win. That's the definition of performance-based love and is the kind of love the world gives—but is the exact opposite of the love of Jesus Christ.

If your mentee won't receive your help and love, more times than not it is not a shot at you. Rather, it is a lack of experience in people helping them. They've had to survive on their own for so long with no one to depend on. Then someone says they want help—and there's no strings attached? A lot of kids simply don't know how to handle that.

If your mentee does not follow your advice, maybe it's because they want to prove how smart and capable they are by doing it their way. It's not that they think your advice is bad (most of the time) but the fact they've never had anyone give them advice before and they don't know what to do with it. Maybe it's pride and lack of submission that stem from past hurts.

Does your mentee not receive your praise? It drives me crazy when I give someone a compliment and they reject it.

"Hey, great job on your paper," I say.

"Well, I didn't really do anything. It's no big deal."

I stare at them and say, "Well, if you didn't do anything, then who wrote the paper?"

Silence.

"Dude, it's okay to allow someone to compliment you," I'll say. "It's a good thing to accept praise about what you do and who you are. Don't deflect it. You can say 'thank you' when someone says nice things about you."

Do they not respond to your phone calls or texts? Will they not let you hug them or show any type of physical affection? It took me a long time before I could finally hug Chris.

Inability to receive is an obstacle that can stunt mentoring relationships. When the mentee rejects your efforts, it is easy to feel demoralized.

Trust Issues

Any parent will tell you it's difficult to get a kid to open up. A one-word answer coming from a kid with eyes glued to the phone seems to be the norm. Imagine how much harder is it for kids who have experienced trauma to trust a mentor they just met?

Trusting adults can be especially difficult on a child who has been hurt by a trusted adult. Whether it's because of a father who said he'd never leave, or an abusive family member, it's hard to trust any adult when you've experienced broken trust. Keeping themselves closed off is a protection mechanism.

When a mentee chooses to share important issues going on in his or her life, it is both good and risky. It's good because you have the opportunity to support, encourage, and love the child through your response. But it's risky because you now could hurt them through your response.

When a child does not open up and share the innermost parts of their life with you, it is easy to believe they either don't like you or don't need you. This is not true. Patience is needed. Sometimes it takes years to develop an authentic relationship full of truth and vulnerability. Some kids have spent years building their wall of self-protection and it can take years to deconstruct that wall as well.

Inability to Forgive

Lack of trust plays right into the inability to forgive.

The enemy is constantly lying to the mentee in order to destroy the relationship. He whispers, "You cannot trust anyone. If you do, they will hurt you."

This is a big deal because the truth is we will fail the kids we mentor. There will come a time we forget to show up or we say the wrong thing. We will unintentionally hurt them in some way. This gives the enemy an open door to attack the relationship. This puts mentors in a tough spot because it almost forces us to be perfect—and perfect according to the standards of the mentee, be they realistic or unrealistic.

Combine the lies with past experiences of broken trust and there is a tendency to assume the worst about people. This makes the enemy's lies very believable. Mentees will rarely give you the benefit of the doubt and constantly look for anything that even remotely resembles a threat, or reason, to break trust. Relationships are often cut off at the first sign of trouble and isolation ensues.

It is natural to get frustrated with your mentee if the child is holding a grudge against you for a seemingly minor error. And although this is definitely an obstacle in mentoring relationships, the inability to forgive will impact your mentee in every relationship. How are they going to respond when their boss hurts their feelings or when a miscommunication with a friend causes disunity? What about when their spouse says something rude out of frustration or when someone they care about makes a mistake?

The Bible is clear about the importance of forgiveness. Expecting perfection and holding grudges in relationships will guarantee disappointment, isolation, and loneliness. And both of those things will keep your mentee from becoming all the Lord has for the child.

Identity

Identity is how you see yourself. A lot of the kids I know have a pretty low view of themselves. They don't believe they are valued for who they are, can do anything, nor do they think they are smart or talented. Despite their best efforts to cover this up, deep down they lack confidence and self-worth, especially when things don't go their way. This is exactly the plan of the enemy.

When trauma occurs, it offers the enemy the perfect opportunity to whispers lies like, "no one loves you" and "if you were good enough, this wouldn't have happened." These lies affect the thing which matters most: identity. A mentee's inner dialogue changes from, "I made a mistake," to "I am a mistake." It goes from, "This person doesn't love me," to "I am unlovable." Our kids once thought, "I failed at this," and now they think, "I am a failure." These lies are subtle, but they make a massive impact. Guilt and shame lead to depression.

If our mentees don't believe they are smart, why would they engage in school? If they don't believe they are lovable, why would they allow a mentor to build a relationship with them? If they believe they are a failure, why try at anything?

This is why suicide, depression, and substance abuse are real things for mentees. I've had to talk a sixth grader out of taking his own life and I've watched a kid melt down while screaming, "I'm a bad kid. No one will ever love me." A child has very little chance of fighting back against the lies of the enemy unless someone helps them in the battle.

Communication Barriers

Bryce is a mentor. He was doing a fantastic job building a relationship with Jacob—showing up every week to hang out with Jacob and starting to see fruit. That is until one day, out of nowhere, Jacob moved. Of course, this was a blow to Bryce who really enjoyed being a mentor. He didn't even get to say goodbye to Jacob.

Moving obviously disrupts a mentoring relationship. With poverty and instability comes a higher rate of relocation. It is hard to hang out with a child if you do not live in the same city. For Chris, one of the main reasons he wanted to stay with my wife and me is because he was tired of moving. By the time he was in eighth grade, he had already been to half a dozen schools.

There can also be changes in cell phone numbers or a cell service being disconnected. I've seen many mentoring relationships dissolve because the mentor simply cannot contact the kid or his family.

These communication barriers aren't as serious as fear or anger, but they can disrupt a mentoring relationship, nonetheless.

. . .

Other Obstacles

If there is one thing you can count on in mentoring, it is the enemy doing whatever he can to come between you and your mentee. He wants to divide your relationship and make it seem like you and your mentee are too far apart on too many issues for this relationship to work.

I have seen the enemy try to split up mentoring relationships because of differing views on political parties and voting preferences. I have seen walls go up because of race issues and how one person sees today's social climate. Sexual orientation has become an issue as well when mentors are puzzled about how they can agree to disagree with their mentee. Entertainment and music preferences, hobbies, and family values are other areas the enemy will use cause division with your mentee.

The bottom line is the enemy wants you to believe that you have nothing in common with your mentee, you are too different from him or her to make an impact, and this relationship is a lost cause due to your differences. All of these are lies.

These and more obstacles to mentoring can feel overwhelming. It can seem like there is no hope. But let me assure you that is exactly what the enemy wants you to believe.

If a mentee is stricken with fear and doesn't believe anyone could love them, they need you to introduce them to the One who is perfect love, the One who casts out fear, and loves no matter what. The love of Jesus shown through you, your words, and your actions is enough to overcome any mentoring obstacle.

Every child needs someone in their life who will champion and support them. They need someone they can depend on; someone they can trust. This provides the security needed to flourish and reach their God-given potential. They are looking for someone to encourage them, to open their heart, cultivate their inner courage, help them face their past, and see themselves as Jesus sees them.

You don't have to be perfect, but you can point them to the perfect One. You might not be able to change them, but you can love them and pray for them. For some kids, they have no one on earth who does that for them. Think about that for a second.

It is only through a relationship with Christ things such as fear, anger, and insecurity are conquered. And our kids need someone who can emulate the person of Christ and introduce them to a relationship with Him.

Jesus loves these kids. He is crystal clear when He says He is a Father to the fatherless and near to the brokenhearted (Psalm 68:5). He wants to give orphan a seat at His table as His child. In His kindness, He wants to use people like me and you to feed and care for His sheep. He wants us to be generous to the poor and to give freedom to the oppressed. He wants His faithful servants to make it their life mission to love the unlovable and to befriend the lonely.

God is looking for the faithful—people who will say "yes" in the midst of uncertainty and fear. He is looking for someone like you.

CHAPTER FOUR

The Mindset of a Mentor

MY MENTOR, STEVE ALLEN, spent sixteen years on the mission field in Bangkok, Thailand. Steve and his wife, Samantha, joyfully sacrificed those years ministering to an unfamiliar people group. They experienced persecution and honor, witnessed life transformation and endured heartache. The journey was difficult, but the experience was worth it.

Heeding a call to the mission field is a big deal, and one would be wise to prepare for such a journey. If one does not respect the call and prepare as they should, they will not only hurt themselves, but others as well.

For Steve and Samantha, preparing for the mission field meant spending four years at a Christian college learning about being a missionary. Once they received their degrees, they sat under a missionary mentor in for three years, training how to spread the Gospel to an unbeliever. They learned the Thai language and Thai culture. They surrounded themselves with other experienced missionaries and filled their time learning through books and interviews. Looking back, Steve and Samantha credit this preparation and the hard work they put in initially as the cause for the longevity of their ministry.

In a similar way, it's easy to think if you've had success as a parent or in the business world, that same success will translate in a mentoring relationship. But this kind of thinking has sabotaged many mentoring relationships even before they start. Mentoring, and the child you are investing into, requires your respect and full attention. The road to a successful mentoring relationship starts with humility and a willingness to learn.

Obviously, going to Thailand and mentoring a kid from across town are vastly different experiences, but there are similarities. After all, kids from hard places have a different culture and speak a different language. The things they care about aren't necessarily the things we care about. You might not even be the same race or religion or even in the same social class. To be an effective mentor, the first thing a mentor needs to have is the correct mindset.

Here are some things to help you stay in the mentoring game for the long haul:

There is No Such Thing as a Bad Kid

In my experience, I can't think of a more toxic environment than the junior high teacher's lounge at the school where I used to work. It was a cesspool of negativity, gossip, and slander. Not all the teachers participated, but the same few always seemed to be in there and it felt like they never stopped complaining about the children they taught. One particular phrase really made me furious: "Oh, he's just a bad kid."

This could have been said about Chris and the choices he made. But let's take a closer look:

- Perhaps Chris didn't trust us because he was abandoned by his father and separated from his mother, the person he loved most in this world.
- Maybe Chris didn't respect male authority because multiple men had come in and out of his life for as long as he could remember, and some were abusive to him and his mother.
- Jail might not have seemed a big deal to Chris because two of his older brothers were already incarcerated.
- Maybe the reason he had sex with his girlfriend was because the only thing in life he really wanted was to be loved and

accepted.

- Despite his silence, Chris had a lot to say. But perhaps he was just terrified to trust that anyone would actually listen.
- The trauma from moving every two years and not having a community, friend base, or family might have been catching up to him and why he acted the way he did.

Let me ask you this: when the Lord looks down from heaven and sees Chris, what does He think? I can tell you what He doesn't think: He doesn't think Chris is a bad kid. Chris is God's workmanship who has a ton of value in His eyes. Jesus Christ came and died on the cross just for Chris. He is wonderfully and fearfully made. I can imagine the Lord's heart breaks for a child like Chris who has experienced so much pain already in his life.

Chris is a hurt kid. His actions are a result of the experiences he went through. Fear and insecurity will force any human to do what they must do to get their needs met and survive.

When a kid is acting his worst is when he needs love the most. Their actions are saying something—something they can't articulate or put into words.

There is Always a Reason Why

There is always a reason why a person acts the way they do. It is up to us as mentors, as mature adults who love and follow Jesus, to figure out the why behind the actions of our kids. When you figure out the why, compassion replaces judgement.

We have the opportunity to become an expert on the kids we mentor. But before kids will open up to you, they must feel safe around you. They will only feel safe when they trust you, and they never flippantly give their trust. First, you must work for it.

Over time, children will drop little clues as to the why behind their behavior. We must be on the lookout for those chances to invite and encourage them to share more by asking follow-up questions, one at a time. From there, it is up to them if they want to share or not. Just as the Lord does with us, we as mentors can only invite and then wait for a child to reply when they are ready. This cannot be forced.

Earn the Right to Be Heard

I remember my first day of school as a teacher. Although I had a degree in education and some student teaching under my belt, nothing prepared me to be in charge of a classroom by myself. I was terrified. Thirty sets of eyes were glued on me and I had no clue what I was doing.

Junior high students are fairly similar to wild animals: they can smell fear and will take advantage if they think you are weak. They even have a tendency to gang up and attack in packs. I tried my hardest to be strict and authoritative on that first day. It backfired in a major way.

It started with a simple request. "Can everyone please take out some paper and a pencil?" That's when Jacari made his presence known with a "Nope!" the entire class heard. I looked over and snapped back, "Who said that?"

The class froze.

Now I was in trouble. Someone had clearly defied my authority and he was making me look like an idiot. Even worse, I had asked a question in which any rational student would never answer.

I spotted the one kid who didn't have a pencil or paper on his desk.

I went over to him and said, "I asked you to take out a pencil and paper."

"And I said nope." He slouched in his desk. "Look man, I don't know you and you don't know me. Why should I do what you tell me to do? You better get real first before you come in here barking orders."

I'll never forget it. Jacari quickly became one of my favorite students. We ended up having a great relationship, but I had to show I was trustworthy.

The saying goes, "You must earn the right to be heard." A kid doesn't care what you know until he knows you care.

Knowing you care creates an environment of safety in which the child can feel heard and respected. Before they share their story with you, they need to know they can trust you. Earning their trust takes time as they need to be sure you are for real and you won't hurt them. They first need to know you see them as an individual and care for them as a person.

How quickly trust is grown is dependent on your actions, how you react to their behavior and their past. Typically, the younger the child is, the fewer walls they've built. The older they are, the longer it takes to earn the right to be heard because that wall of protection is built pretty high.

Having a hard conversation or giving advice before a child is ready to hear you can set your relationship back a long way if it goes poorly. Every child is different because each one's background is different. For some kids, it takes months, maybe even years, to earn their trust.

All Frustration Comes From Unmet Expectations

A saying that rings true especially when mentoring kids from hard places is, "All frustration comes from unmet expectations."

Unfortunately, mentors have a vision of what they want their mentee to become, and often it's based on the mentor's vision of success. You want your mentee to go to college, get a job, wear a suit, and get married because you went to college, got a job, wore a suit, and got married. But what if your mentee doesn't want to go to college? What if instead of a suit and high-and-tight haircut, he prefers baggy jeans and dreadlocks? Will you be disappointed?

On average, success is recognized as:

- Academic achievements
- Dressing nicer
- Athletic success
- No drugs, alcohol, or premarital sex
- Better behavior
- No cussing
- Going to church
- Showing kindness
- Being polite and respectful

Don't get me wrong, these are all good things. There is nothing wrong with giving your mentee the option to do as you have done. But your way is one way, it is not *the* way. We must be careful not to get caught up trying to get them to emulate us instead of Christ.

Your mentee is different than you. He or she has a different story, different skills, and a different personality than you. Work with your mentee to figure out what God's unique, individual call and plan is for him or her.

Focus instead on making disciples of Christ. The first step is letting go of the expectations you have for your mentee. As hard as it may be, don't focus on the end results. Instead, focus on the process of showing up and loving them right where they are.

When our expectations aren't met, frustration sets in. When negativity enters your relationship, the enemy uses it to wreak havoc on the trust you've built together. It's okay to hope your mentee goes to college or has athletic success, but don't expect it. Expectation is rigid, but hope is flexible. Expectation is assuming something will happen. Hope is wishing or desiring good to happen. Don't bury your mentee with the weight of having to live up to your expectations.

Believe the Best

Comparing your mentoring relationship with other mentor-mentee relationships is a dangerous trap set by the enemy and a quick way to get discouraged.

Comparison also leads you to focus on the negative, on what is *not* happening, instead of the good things that *are* happening. Negativity is a contagious disease, affecting everyone around. It causes gossip and slander while destroying hope. The enemy knows if he can get you complaining then the next step is hopelessness.

Hopelessness is the belief that this isn't working, nor will it ever work. This causes a mentor to quit investing in the life of their mentee. If a mentor comes to believe change is not possible, why continue?

The enemy wants you to believe your mentee didn't show up because he doesn't like you. He wants you to think your mentee didn't answer your text because she doesn't need you. He plants the thought that because your mentee failed a class, he or she will be a failure in life. The enemy whispers, "That kid doesn't appreciate you, respect you, or need you."

Don't fall for it. Don't get sucked into his lies. We are mentoring children, not adults. They will forget to show up and they won't always be responsive. They will make mistakes and bad decisions. They will prioritize hanging out with their friends and playing video games over hanging out with you. They will say things like, "I hate you," or "I don't want to hang out with you." Give them some time. Let things cool down. Keep pursuing, be consistent, and ask the hard questions.

Fixate On the Good, Not the Bad

Jamal was a mentee in our program and a natural leader. He was funny, easy to be around, and truly determined to make something out of his life. Even though he was supremely intelligent and talented, he lacked self-confidence in himself. He needed a lot of praise and encouragement from others. He also had quite the temper and would explode at his peers when things didn't go his way.

When I encounter a kid like Jamal and see his potential, I think, "If this kid can just improve in a few areas, the sky's the limit for him. I'm going to get to work on him and see how I can help." But this is similar to a sports coach finding a prospect who can jump the highest and run the fastest but has never learned how to play the sport.

I started to spend more time with Jamal and thought I was doing a good thing when I told him the ways he needed to get better. That's not how Jamal saw it, though. What I was trying to do and what Jamal was experiencing were not aligned.

One day, I pulled Jamal into my office after he was acting up in our program. I asked him how he was doing and what was going on.

"Nothing is going on. Everything is fine," he responded.

I chalked it up to him just having a bad day, so I seized the opportunity to ask him about his failing grade in math. After I gave him a lecture about how grades are important and how he needs to do better, Jamal said something which rocked me to my core.

"Do I ever do anything right?"

"Well, of course you do, Jamal. You do a lot of things right," I said.

"Then how come you never talk about those things and you just always talk about what I'm doing wrong?"

I had been too busy trying to improve Jamal that I totally missed encouraging him in all the good things he was doing. While he was having a hard time in math class, he was improving his attitude, his actions toward others, and controlling his anger. The truth is, he had grown tremendously over the past semester. But I missed it because I was fixated on what he was doing wrong instead of what he was doing right.

You're going to be a lot more effective as a mentor if you focus on the good things instead of harping on the bad things. Of course, there is always a time for correction. But if you find yourself rebuking more than encouraging, the mentoring relationship will not succeed. If a kid is doing ninety-nine things wrong and one thing right, focus on the one thing.

Mentoring is a marathon. Trust the Lord to address the ninety-nine things. You just love your mentee where he or she is at and encourage him in the progress being made.

***

As mentors, we are fighting a battle for the soul of our mentees. We are soldiers called by the Lord to help our kids know the Lord and become all God has made them to be. The battle starts with our mindset—how we perceive our mentee, what we believe about them, and what the voice inside our head is saying when we think of them.

When thinking about our mentee, have the mind of Christ. My prayer is, "Lord, give me eyes to see my mentee the way You see them." Instead of seeing them as the world sees them, we can transform our thinking to discern God's will for our mentee.

Think on the good. Protect your mind from any complaining, grumbling, or comparison. Trust the Lord is working, even if you can't see it. If there is anything worthy of praise in the life of your mentee, think about those things.

CHAPTER FIVE

The Focus of a Mentor

CARLOS WAS THE first mentee in our Forerunner Mentor Program. A brilliant student, a magnetic personality, and a hard worker who desired to improve his life, all packed into one kid. But, when we first met Carlos, he was none of those things. When I approached him to see if he wanted a mentor, he was a little hesitant to agree. I remember him saying, "So this mentor is a total stranger and I'm just supposed to hang out with him? Sounds a little weird to me."

Funny, I was thinking the same thing.

Slowly but surely, we saw some improvements in Carlos. His mentor, Peter, did a great job of spending time with Carlos. Peter encouraged Carlos, showed up to his games, and built a relationship with Carlos's whole family. During Carlos's nineth grade year, Carlos really focused on his grades and made the National Honors Society. In tenth and eleventh grade, Carlos set his sights on wrestling and became the team captain. His senior year was filled with SAT testing, prom, and graduation. Next stop: college.

Since then, Carlos has flourished in college. He is making tremendous grades while working multiple jobs and participating in extra-curricular activities. He has even set himself up with a job after college through summer internships.

We couldn't be more proud of Carlos. Every time I hear his name, I smile.

Wouldn't it be great if all mentees turned out like Carlos? Peter can hold his head high and say, "I made a positive impact. Carlos wouldn't be where he is today if it wasn't for our relationship." And he would be right. We can safely say the mentoring relationship between Carlos and Peter is successful.

But what if Peter's efforts didn't cause Carlos to enroll in college and a full-time job? What if Carlos wasn't the captain of the wrestling team? What if he made mediocre grades? What if he dropped out of college? Would the relationship still be considered successful then?

You can be the best mentor and your mentee can still not fulfill his potential. There is no automatic guarantee your child will have worldly success. You cannot control the decisions another human being makes, no matter how much you care about them.

One of my favorite sayings in mentoring is, "You can lead a horse to water, but you can't make him drink." You can't force a mentee to take advantage of your generosity or wisdom. After all, "the fear of the Lord is the beginning of knowledge; but fools despise wisdom and instruction" (Proverbs 1:7, NIV). Not to call your mentee a fool, but I think it's safe to say all children and teenagers act in foolish ways from time to time.

There is simply no magic formula in mentoring. But there is a formula to create a setting for which the Lord can show up and do what He does best. We make terrible saviors, but that's precisely what God does best. We as mentors can have a front-row seat to watch Him work, but we must stay in the game. Our focus as mentors needs to be on what we can control through the following three actions: invest, love, and trust.

Invest

You might not always see it, but God is always working behind the scenes. He who calls you is faithful. And that requires sacrificial investment from us. Here are some ways we can invest into the life of our mentees:

We Invest Our Time

Time is one of the most important things we have. Time is also the most important ingredient to relationships. Without time, your relationship is likely to suffer. But time is a finite resource, as we only have so much of it in each day.

My first year of marriage, like many husbands before me, I made it my goal to be the best husband ever. I would do the dishes, walk the dog, do the laundry, and mow the grass. I ran myself ragged buying my wife flowers and gift cards, writing letters, and buying her gift cards for pedicures and manicures. I was constantly doing things for her to prove my love for her.

At first, she loved it and our marriage flourished. But after a while, things cooled off. I didn't understand what the problem was, especially with all of the things I was doing for her.

One night, my wife sat next to me on the couch as I was folding laundry. She said, "You know Zach, I really appreciate you cleaning and buying me stuff. But all I really want is to spend time with you. The other stuff can go out the window if I can't truly be with you."

Relationships are the vehicles the Lord uses to change lives, and time is the gasoline that makes those vehicles run. You spend the most of your time with the people who mean the most to you. Time tells others they are worthy of your investment. It shows them they matter and you care about them. In our Forerunner Mentoring Program, the most fruitful relationships tend to be the ones where the most time is invested.

Jesus knew true impartation comes from spending time with one another. He spent time with His disciples, day in and day out. He spent His time with people, investing in them, and giving everything He had to them. They would then pass on what they learned to the rest of the world. Jesus knew living life together was the best way to spread the Gospel.

My friend John knew this principal, too. He was the first person to mentor me once I gave my life to Christ. Although the two of us are the same age, John was much further in his walk with Jesus than I was. I would not be here today if it wasn't for John's investment in my life. Every Thursday morning for over three years, the two of us would meet. John had a demanding job, a wife, and a kid of his own. He definitely didn't have time to spare. But he made time. John made time to meet me for breakfast once a week and invest in my life. Sometimes we'd meet as early as 5 a.m. because of his hectic schedule. He invited me over to his house to be with his wife and family. Anytime they had a gathering at their house, he invited me. And that made all the difference. He earned the right to be heard and I grew to trust and love him.

A friend once said, "The only two things that matter in life is the Word of God and the souls of man." John sacrificed his time to invest in my soul. The Lord used John not only to change my life, but the lives of my sons, my wife, and every person who comes in contact with me. You never know what the Lord is going to do with the time you invest into the life of a child. He might use it to impact generation after generation.

We Invest Our Energy

On most days, I feel like there is too much to do and not enough hours in the day. There seems to be a million things fighting for our energy: work, family, hobbies, sleep, friendships, church, and the list goes on and on. It feels like I run out of energy on Wednesday about 3:00 in the afternoon. I am often completely spent by the end of the week.

Mentoring is another thing to add to your calendar. You must find the energy to commit to mentoring somewhere in the middle of your jam-packed life. But when you give your energy for your mentee, the Lord has a habit of blessing your sacrifice like crazy. The Bible tells us not to neglect to do good and to share what you have, for such sacrifices are pleasing to God (Hebrews 13:16). Just like the story of Jesus feeding the five thousand, you'll be amazed at what the Lord can do with your small margins.

I started mentoring a kid named Villy when he was in eighth grade. He was a great kid who refused to back down from any challenge. Laid back and quiet, it was easy to miss him in a crowd of people.

I tried to find a mentor for Villy, but had the hardest time finding someone to commit. Finally, acting either out of pride or out of obedience to the Lord, I said I'd mentor Villy. From the get-go, this seemed like a bad idea due to my busy schedule. I had just gotten married, I had a kid on the way, and a growing organization to focus on. I just didn't have the energy to invest in Villy the way he deserved. For the first few years, I saw him once every couple of months. As he got into high school, it turned into once every quarter. By his senior year, I think I saw him three times that year. Even when I did show up, I had almost nothing to offer him either because I was tired or busy thinking about something else. I wasn't winning any "mentor of the year" awards in my relationship with Villy.

Things only got worse as he got older. Sure, I'd call and text him, but my communication was fairly limited with Villy. I believed the enemy's lies that I was a terrible mentor. I even let my guilt and shame keep me from seeing him on multiple occasions. I admit I was an awful mentor to Villy, but he was doing really well in life. He had good grades, played varsity football, and was the first one in his family to go to college.

Right before he left for his new life as a college student, I took Villy out to dinner. We mostly just caught up, talked about sports, and reminisced about old junior high football memories. As our conversation died down, Villy got real serious with me. He looked me in the eyes and told me how thankful he was for my role in his life. He said he was proud to tell people I was his mentor. He even said he wouldn't be where he is today without my influence.

I was floored. I don't know if I can recall a time when I felt more honored. I had been thinking I was a terrible mentor. And by all accounts, I was a terrible mentor. But the Lord used my small sacrifice and multiplied it. I didn't have much energy to devote to Villy, but the Lord still used what I had to impact his life. He turned my little investment into a big gain for Villy.

It is important for us as mentors to take care of ourselves and make sure we are filled up so we can pour out. But we also know seasons of difficulty come along from time to time. There will be days when we show up even though we are tired, call when we're running on empty, or only have enough energy to send a text on the way home from work. Know the Lord will use these investments to change a life. God can take our little and turn it into a lot.

· · ·

We Invest Our Prayers

One of my school counselor friends called the other day saying a boy was having a hard time lately. His family moved from Jamaica and were adjusting well to life in the United States. His mom worked at a hospital and his father had an early morning shift at a local store. The son was making good grades and fitting in well socially and academically. Things seemed to be working out well for this family. But one morning, the father was walking to his car to go to work when someone pulled up, shot and killed him, and stole his car. The incident devastated this family.

As I listened to this story, I could hear the school counselor's heart for this family. She deeply cared for them and was trying to help this family any way she could. She was an advocate for them. "Will you help this family?" she asked me.

When you pray for someone, you are reaching out to God and saying, "Lord, I really care about this person. Would you please help them?" God tells us to keep on praying for all the Lord's people (Ephesians 6:18). He says the prayers of a righteous person has great power (James 6:16). When we pray, it gets our eyes off ourselves and onto Him. And we serve a God who loves to step in and rescue. God loves it when we ask for help.

A little prayer here and there doesn't seem like much, but we must realize our prayers carry great weight. We serve a faithful God who loves to hear our prayers. We have an opportunity to be the only one in the world to call on the Lord and say, "Will you please help this child?"

We Invest Our Love

One of our main focuses is to love our mentee with the love of Christ. Our love comes with no strings attached. We love because He first loved us (1 John 4:19). We love no matter what. Our love is not based on if the child makes good grades, or if they act right.

Performance-based love has no place in mentoring. Performance-based love brings fear and leads to thoughts like, "I don't want to see my mentor because I don't want to get in trouble for failing my math test," or "I don't like my mentor because he's always telling me to act better."

Regrettably, I've been that mentor. More than a few times my actions have left a kid wondering if I love them only when they perform how I want them to perform. My intentions were good, but fear of my mentees not fulfilling their potential caused me to be an ineffective mentor.

My desire is to love like Jesus because He offers us perfect love and perfect love casts out all fear (1 John 4:18). Like the father of the prodigal son, we must embrace these children of God regardless of what they have done and where they have been (Luke 15:11-32). Like Jesus, we as mentors are called to love unconditionally and joyfully.

One of the most common things I hear when someone considers volunteering to mentor is, "I just don't have much to offer. I'm not cool. I don't have anything in common with young people. I just don't think it'll work out." But a mentor doesn't have to be cool. They don't have to know the latest music or the newest dance moves. They don't have to be an athlete or successful or smart. They just have to love. At the end of the day, that's all our kids want—to be loved, just like you and I want to be loved. To a kid who has never been loved, even the tiniest amount of love can transform his or her life.

As a former teacher and coach in a high-poverty area, I came across a lot of kids who were hard to love. I can remember being absolutely appalled at the kids' behavior during my first few years teaching.

Jayden especially got under my skin. He was your typical class clown and would do anything, and I mean anything, to get the attention of his peers. He would make fun of people, scream out cuss words, steal things, and try his hardest to make his peers laugh at him. I feel like I was a pretty patient teacher and generally liked most kids, but I couldn't stand Jayden. Every time I saw him, I caught a bad mood.

That summer, I volunteered to be a small group leader on a hiking trip in Colorado for a para-church ministry at our school. Jayden was in my small group. It was my job to keep an eye on him and ten of his friends. I had to sit by Jayden on the bus, eat my meals with him, and live with him for a week.

On our way to Colorado, we had to pull over in Amarillo, Texas at 3 a.m. because of some bus issues. Lucky for us, we had a church connection and were able to unload all 300 kids to get some sleep while the bus was fixed.

So, there we were, all 300 of us crammed in a church youth room trying to get some sleep. Everyone was quiet except for Jayden. He was making annoying sounds and trying to make people laugh. But he was keeping the other kids and adults awake, and they were getting upset. After about 45 minutes of this, I pulled him outside and told him just what I thought of him and his antics. After I was done, he looked me square in the face and said, "Why do you hate me so much?"

His words shook me. I realized it was time to do some soul searching and find out why I felt so judgmental toward Jayden.

After that confrontation, I did my best to ignore Jayden and keep my distance. I just tried to get through the week without having to deal with him again.

One of the trip activities was to split into small groups and share our testimonies. Typically, I am not a real big fan of sharing testimonies. But there is something about being in the middle of nowhere that brings out the vulnerability and authenticity in high schoolers. I truly enjoyed hearing my student's stories. By the last day, everyone had gone except Jayden. I remember how I felt right before he shared. I wanted him to get this over with as fast as possible because I was certain he wouldn't take it seriously. I was not looking forward to hearing him share.

But Jayden's story was one I will never forget. He shared he was adopted. He honored his adoptive parents and spoke highly of them, but the only thing in life he really wanted was to be loved by his biological mother and father. He wanted his family back together. Jayden shared about his anger toward the father he had never met. He told how his mother gave birth to him in prison and how, even though he had never met her, and she was still in prison, he loved her. He then broke down crying because he had just found out his mother passed away in prison due to an illness. He never got the chance to meet her.

I cried as Jayden shared his story. After he was finished, I remember the Lord telling me, "Zach, there is always a reason why a kid acts the way he does. He is not a bad kid; he is a hurt kid. You get to love him in the midst of his pain."

Jayden acted the way he did because he was abandoned by his parents, was unable to receive love from his biological parents, and processing the loss of his mother and the dream he had of meeting her face-to-face. Once I realized that, my love for Jayden grew.

Jesus calls us to love. He doesn't say love *if*, He says to love *no matter what*. Kids can be hard to love. Hurt kids can be even harder to love. But there is always a reason why he or she is hard to love. If you are mentoring a kid who has been dealt a tough hand, I can promise you it will be hard at times. They will dishonor you, disobey you, and keep you at arm's length. They will give you every reason in the book to not love them.

This is often what we do with the Lord. We dishonor the Lord with our actions, disobey Him with our decisions and keep Him at arm's length when He tries to help. But He is always there for us with a love-you-no-matter-what kind of love.

Just like Jesus, we're here to love unconditionally. When we agree to mentor kids, we are saying nothing—not their actions, their words, their past, their behavior—will be able to separate us from loving them.

We Invest Our Trust

When I first started to mentor, I thought it was my job to fix a kid. I took a lot of pride in being the one who could transform a kid's life. I thought I had all the right ingredients to take a kid who had been dealt a tough hand and turn him into a success story. That's why I didn't blink when Chris's mother asked my wife and I to be his guardians.

Looking back, I can see the pride in my ways. My prideful mind thought Chris was lucky to have me. My thought process was something along the lines of "Just wait until I get ahold of him. He'll be making straight A's and on his way to college in no time." Instead of pointing Chris to the Savior, I tried to be his savior. And I make a terrible savior.

I believed my relationship with Chris was like a math equation: if I invest and I love, then he will be transformed. But thinking I am the one who transforms is contrary to the way the Lord operates. The Lord asks us to invest what we have. He urges us to love no matter what. And He asks we trust Him to transform a life in His perfect timing.

No one, not even Jesus, had a 100 percent success rate discipling people (remember Judas?). Sometimes we see fruit, other times we don't. But God is way more concerned about our obedience to His call and to trust that He loves these kids more than we do.

It is not up to us to transform our mentees. We were not created to carry that weight. It is not our job. That job belongs to God. Our job to trust that God will move in His perfect time. Only God knows what is truly going on in a kid's heart. Yes, He can work through you and can use you to plant and water the seeds of growth. But ultimately, it is up to Him.

You invest. You love. You trust the Lord with the transformation.

In the 1970s, Ben and Emily started volunteering with a para-church junior high ministry which served a low-income area of our community. Every Sunday night, they had the same twelve boys over to their house for pizza and a Bible study. The boys loved them, even going so far as to call them their second mom and dad. This went on for years and soon the boys turned into men entering their final year of high school. Ben and Emily came to love these boys as their own and would do anything to serve them. During the Bible studies, the boys would listen, ask questions, and pray for each other. A few of the kids even got baptized. Every kid was engaged, except for one kid named Scottie.

Scottie showed up every week to Ben and Emily's house, but never said a word. He wouldn't say thank you, wouldn't let Ben or Emily into his life, and he never shared anything when it was time for prayer requests. As the young men graduated high school and went their separate ways, Ben and Emily felt like they truly made an impact with eleven of the kids. They just missed it with Scottie.

Fast forward a few years and Ben was on his way home from work when his gas light came on. He had to pull over quick to fill up. The problem was he was on the wrong side of the neighborhood. Having no other choice, Ben drove his freshly washed Honda Accord to the filling station. Ben was fueling his car when he heard someone yelling.

The voice kept getting louder and louder and Ben realized there was a six foot, six inch, three-hundred pound man coming his way. Ben tried his best to ignore him, but there was no ignoring this man.

"Hey, man. I got a question for you," the large man said.

"Uh yes, go ahead," replied Ben.

"Is your name Ben Lawson?"

"Uh, yes…"

"Hey, man, I just wanted you to know not a day goes by I don't think about you. I couldn't say it back then because I was so shy, but I just wanted to say thank you. I'm a married man with three kids of my own now, and everything I learned about being a husband and a father I learned by watching you those Sunday nights at your house."

"Well, thanks," said Ben, dumbfounded. "I'm sorry, what did you say your name was?"

"It's me, Ben. Scottie!"

For thirty years, Ben and Emily thought they had missed it with Scottie. They invested, they loved, but they thought they had failed because they didn't see the fruit. The enemy used the lack of obvious results to lie to them that they failed with Scottie.

But God did transform Scottie's heart. God always uses your investment—it just might not be in your timing.

Paul writes in 1st Corinthians 1:6-7, "I planted, Apollos watered, but God gave the growth. So neither he who plants nor he who waters is anything, but only God who gives the growth" (ESV). Trust is the name of the game in mentoring. Let us learn to trust that God will not let our investment or love return void. Regardless of if we see the fruit or not, we trust God is at work.

CHAPTER SIX

The Job of a Mentor

OUR NUMBER ONE job as a mentor is to produce followers of God. Success in academics, athletics, professionalism, and maturity are all good. But a good jump shot, nice looking haircut, and making all A's in math class aren't going to deepen your mentee's relationship with the Lord. Would you rather your mentee be a garbage man who loves Jesus with all his heart, or a doctor who doesn't know Jesus? Most mentors would say the garbage man, but what do our actions say? Do we spend more time trying to improve our mentees' chances of getting a good job than we are ensuring they know Jesus Christ on a personal level? You can tell what a person truly cares about by seeing where he spends his time and his money—and that goes for his mentoring relationships as well.

We are here to help our mentees become followers of Christ, knowing His true character and nature, be secure in their identity, and serve those around them. Within this job, there are three objectives:

Objective #1: Show Up

When an adult shows up in the life of a child, it communicates to the child that they are valuable. Mentors show up in two ways, by pursuing their mentee and by being present.

Pursuit

The first group of men who pursued me were my junior high football coaches. They showed up day after day for me. Sure, it was their job, but that didn't matter to me. All that mattered is they were there.

Coach Z was a former minor league baseball player who had a Tom Selleck mustache and arms like lead pipes. I'll never forget how he made me feel when he would go out of his way to say hi to me in the hallways.

My basketball coach, Coach Malcolm, was quick to give me a nickname and invite me to play basketball with him after school during the off-season. I can still hear his voice "Dang it, Hack. You foul more than any other kid I've ever met."

Coach Boone was the cool coach who would call me into his office to hang out and chat like I was one of his good friends.

Those men helped me feel important, special, and like I mattered every time I saw them. Their pursuit of me kept me in athletics, which probably kept me from getting into trouble. I didn't have men in high school who cared for me like these coaches, and that is when I really started to make a mess of my life.

Kids need mentors who show up and pursue them. The choice to relentlessly pursue your mentee through their junk is more important than just about any other quality. It matters more than the color of your skin, your knowledge of current culture, or how cool you are. Our kids are dying for love, and they don't really care who gives it to them. You show them you love them by being in their corner, rain or shine. Sometimes they will intentionally try to push you away or make things difficult because they've been burned in the past. But by fighting for their attention, we can give them a reason to trust again.

God pursues us through our bad decisions, pride, and sin. He is relentless. He never gives up, no matter how long we try to outrun Him. We as mentors follow His example.

. . .

Presence

Big Bill and I met about ten years ago when I coached his son during his eighth grade basketball season. Big Bill looks like a mix between Mr. Clean and the Hulk. He tends to be more business than pleasure and isn't afraid to share his opinion if he thinks you are doing something wrong. His voice is deep and booming. His handshake has probably broken a few bones before.

Picture a first-year junior high basketball coach having Big Bill as a player's parent. Imagine feeling the eyes of this giant of a man staring at you when you don't put his son into the game. It was absolutely terrifying.

Every spring, I make a pitch to our local community for new mentors. I put the word out far and wide and then I wait for applications to flood my inbox. Within a few weeks that spring, I had matched all our mentees except for one—a young man named Eddie.

Eddie was a shy, introverted 10-year-old boy. He was raised by a no-nonsense mom who made sure her son was doing his best in school. Eddie and his mother had just moved to America from Africa so Eddie could get a better education. I was really excited about finding him a mentor.

One day, I received an application from Big Bill. In his application, Big Bill wrote, "I want to contribute to the community and serve by helping to address a major societal problem. As a Christian, I need to heed the call of scripture to take care of widows and orphans."

I just didn't know how Big Bill, a strait-laced, no nonsense man from Memphis, Tennessee would interact with Eddie, a shy Muslim kid from Africa. I feared Bill would be culturally insensitive. I didn't think he would have a thing in common with Eddie. I thought he was too intense, too big, and too old. But do you know what happened?

Big Bill became the most faithful mentor we have. He shows up no matter what. Big Bill's relationship with Eddie flourished. Eddie has gone from the quietest, most insecure kid in class to having a spirited personality, self-confidence, and earning A's and B's. Not only has Big Bill become a role model for Eddie, but he has also been a constant support for his mother and a wonderful friend to me.

What makes Big Bill such a great mentor boils down to one thing:

he shows up. Big Bill is faithful. Even when he is busy, he makes time to see Eddie face-to-face. When he is on the road for work, Big Bill calls or texts. Big Bill does a fantastic job being consistent for his mentee.

Big Bill is faithful because he said he would be. He is a man of his word. When Big Bill said he would mentor Eddie, he meant it. When Big Bill shows up, Eddie feels cared for, heard, and valued. When Big Bill comes on the scene, Eddie's day gets better.

The kids we mentor have learned the hard way how rare it is to have someone show up consistently. They know the world can be a ruthless place and it doesn't show up for you.

As a mentor, we get to simply pass on what Jesus does for us every day. We get to show up. Jesus always shows up for us and He's never too busy. Every time we are in His presence, life gets easier to handle.

Objective #2: Build Up

I know all too well the power negative words can have on a heart. Growing up, I was a spirited child, quick-witted in my responses, a class clown, and generally the life of the party. I was either the teacher's favorite student or worst nightmare, depending on their personality. But as life got harder, I became jaded. I started to act out for attention and I stopped trying in school.

I remember my fourth-grade teacher pointing her finger in my face and yelling, "You're such a bad kid." I remember my eighth-grade art teacher who threatened me with, "I'd call your dad if he was still around." I remember older men at my church scolding me for talking in class and telling their kids, "Don't hang out with Zach Garza. He's nothing but trouble." I remember a college professor telling me and the entire class I wouldn't amount to anything because I fell asleep in her class. These words came from the adults in my life.

I was born with a fairly severe stutter and was an easy target when someone wanted to cut me to the core. I remember being on the playground in sixth grade when my best friends turned on me and started a chant making fun of my stutter. It spread throughout the whole school.

Looking back, I can give grace to all the people who said those words to me. As a someone who works with kids, I know how easy it can be to lose your cool on a kid who is acting out. But boy, did those words hurt me to the core.

The words people speak over young people shapes the way they form their identity. I came to know myself as "Zach, the bad kid" or "Zach, the stutterer." That view continued into adulthood. I figured this was my identity since it seemed everyone agreed it was. It wasn't until Godly men built me up by speaking truth into my life that my identity began to change.

Steve Allen said I was a man of God, a history maker, and a world changer. A man named Larry said I would become what I didn't have and there would be a day when many people said, "He sure did father us well." Don told me he loved me, liked having me around, and he was proud of me.

Their words brought healing to my wounds. Their words built the man I am today. At first, hearing the truth about me was a little awkward. I had a really hard time believing I was a man of God. But after a while, I began to embrace it. I started to yearn for it. Sometimes I would call Steve just to hear him say, "Man of God! How are you?"

Words matter. They truly can bring life or death. As mentors, we have an opportunity to speak God's truth over our mentees. We get to focus on the positive and predict they will have a prosperous and successful future. We will be the most encouraging people our kids will meet. We want to bring joy and laughter and smiles.

Our students need a lot of courage to go against the grain of the situations they're living in and fulfill their potential. Family issues, prior trauma, cultural pressures, and peer pressure can make it really hard for our mentees to improve. But they have you to cheer them on. You can speak words of identity and destiny over your mentees to help keep them going. We might very well be the only ones on the earth calling out the good in them. At any given moment, the accuser may be whispering to our mentee, "You're not good enough" or "you're a bad kid." Kids have told me they genuinely believe they are dumb and have nothing to offer the world.

Our words matter. Our tone matters. Our facial expressions and body language matter.

Let us be intentional in making sure the words we speak to our mentees are encouraging and life-giving. The lies and expectations of this world can quickly tear down the kids we mentor. What an honor to build them up with words of truth and encouragement.

Objective #3: Love God

I'm not much of a handyman. I don't like using hammers and I have a hard time recognizing the difference between a screw and a nail. The worst part about my handyman insecurity is that my wife happens to be extremely handy. When something breaks, my wife fixes it. She has a pink hammer and a wide assortment of anchors and screws. She is Ms. Fix-It.

While I am 92 percent secure in the fact that my wife is more handy than I am, there is one person who simply cannot wrap their mind around this truth—my father. My dad is a real man's man. There isn't anything around the house my dad can't fix. That his son isn't the least bit handy is quite troubling to him. That my wife is handy is downright offensive to him. In fact, one of the ways he tries to get me to be handier is by buying me tools for Christmas. A few years ago, he got me an air compressor. I got the hint.

One year, I made a vow to learn to be handier. And I wanted to start by learning how to use a drill. A few weeks after making this promise, I was at my mom's house and came across a brand-new drill. I immediately thought it was from the Lord. I asked my mom if I could have it and she said yes. I was beyond excited!

My first job was to create another bookshelf for our living room. This one was going to be the bookshelf of all bookshelves. I went to Home Depot to get all the supplies. As I was putting the piece of wood in my minivan, I thought it felt rather heavy. It had to weigh about 50 pounds. I took the piece of wood home, sanded it, stained it, installed brackets on it, and found the perfect spot on my wall to hang it.

I felt so manly. I grabbed some screws, got my drill, and hung this massive piece of wood. It looked pretty good and I was really proud of myself. I called my wife to admire it with me. I took a picture and sent it to my dad. I put a bunch of books on the bookshelf and called it a day.

A few weeks later, my wife and I startled awake at about 1 a.m. by an incredibly loud noise coming from our living room. Terrified, I slowly walked toward the living room, baseball bat in attack position, about to go Barry Bonds on this intruder. As I walked into our living room, I saw complete chaos. Books everywhere. A piece of twelve-foot Cedarwood on my coffee table. Massive holes in the wall. My bookshelf had fallen. My first handyman project was a failure. I guess I wasn't as handy as I thought.

I was spending time with the Lord a few days later and thinking about mentoring. I asked the question, "Lord, how can I equip our mentors with the best tools to love the kids we serve?"

He reminded me of the bookshelf and I pictured the complete mess. I retraced my actions and thought about how the accident occurred when this question popped into my head: "Zach, was the issue with your brand new DeWalt drill?"

"No way," I thought. "That thing is top of the line. There was nothing wrong with the tool."

"Then what was the issue?"

"Oh, man," I thought. "The issue wasn't with the tool at all. The issue was with the one using the tool. I simply didn't know what I was doing."

The Lord was asking me if as a mentor, am I creating a handyman or am I simply providing tools? That's a tough question to answer.

Jesus knew the importance of discipleship. Jesus didn't give the disciples top-of-the-line fishing tools or a new boat. He said, "Come and follow Me. Learn from Me. Be with Me. Watch how I do it. I will teach you how to fish." Relationship is the best way to make a disciple.

More than anything, we want our kids to know and love Jesus Christ with all their hearts. They will learn how to do that by emulating you. More is caught than taught. Your example gives them a roadmap to follow to become a follower of Christ. "Follow me, and I will teach you how to follow Christ."

This isn't a call to be perfect. This isn't a call to have it all together. It is a call to do whatever you can to become more like Jesus, and invite kids you mentor to join you in the journey. It's ok to say, "I need help being humble/less angry/more kind. I want to look more like Jesus in this area. Would you like to join me?"

Having an intimate relationship with the Lord Jesus Christ is vital. As a mentor, you cannot give away what you don't have. And as you follow Christ, and love Him with all your heart and mind and strength, I am confident the Lord is going to give you everything you need to impact your mentee's life. By fixing our eyes first and foremost on Christ, He will lead you as you lead your mentee.

**

I like to think of myself as a pretty courageous man. I grew up thinking a man shouldn't shy away from anything. As a kid, I thought being scared was for wimps. And even though it is hard to admit, I have been scared a few times in my life. I'm not talking about snakes-and-spiders scared. I'm talking about legitimately terrifying situations.

I am so fortunate God showed His faithfulness through my mentor, Steve. When I was scared about being alone and never getting married, Steve comforted me. When I doubted myself as a leader, Steve reminded me of God's call on my life. When my wife and I experienced two late-term miscarriages, Steve listened and grieved with me. When I called myself a failure, he listened and spoke truth over me. Advice wasn't necessarily what I needed. I needed a friend who didn't give up on me. I needed words to strengthen my inner man. In every season of my life, Steve pursued me, gave me his presence, encouraged me, and provided an example of a man who loved the Lord with his whole heart.

God used Steve as my mentor to change my life. Not by focusing on results, skills, or what I could bring to the relationship. He changed my life through his selflessness. My mentor is the true epitome of a servant-leader. Steve came to serve, not to be served. Showing up, building up, loving God—this is how the Lord used my mentor to transform me. That is the true job of a mentor.

CHAPTER SEVEN

The Heart of a Mentor

FOR THE LONGEST time, my focus in my relationship with Christ was on doing the right thing. My thinking was if I could just muster up the strength to serve, be humble, and forgive—and do it all in the right way—then I'll be like Jesus. I was striving to being perfect. That didn't last long.

As I grew in my relationship with Jesus, the Holy Spirit showed me the importance of my heart. Doing the right things with the wrong heart isn't pleasing to the Lord. Sure, I did the dishes and served my wife, but if I did it with a bad attitude, I missed the point. As a former athlete and get-things-done guy, this was really hard for me to comprehend. I just wanted a to-do list to be like Jesus. I didn't want to have to deal with emotions and motives.

My good friend, Peter Louis, says, "Seriousness is not a fruit of the Holy Spirit." My prayer is that the Lord gives me His heart for my mentee. I want each child to experience Jesus when they hang out with me. I want to consistently be there to the best of my ability and to support them in whatever they are going through. I want my mentee to know I love them, I believe in them, and I am thankful for our relationship.

To do this well, our hearts need to mirror the heart of Jesus. Here's what I mean by that:

Heart of Joy

I have a strong personality and I affect any environment I enter, for better or worse. I also wear my emotions on my sleeve. If I am having a good day, you can see it on my face. You can also tell when I am having a bad day.

Recently, the Lord revealed something to me. I was having a hard time and a fairly chaotic morning when I pulled up to work. I was in a surly mood. As I shut the door to my office, I felt like I needed to spend some time with the Lord.

During my prayer, He asked me, "Zach, do you realize how your mood affects everyone around you?"

I was surprised by this question and pulled one of my trusted employees into my office. I asked him, "What was the mood like before I showed up?"

He told me everyone was laughing and having a good time.

I said, "What about after I showed up?"

He said "Well, things kind of changed when you showed up."

I asked how they changed.

"Sometimes, it just seems like you don't like to be with us."

Wow.

Now, I love my staff. I really do. I consider it my privilege to lead them and would take a bullet for them. But love was not what they were feeling when I walked into the room. They might have known in their heads I loved them, but my actions made them feel like I didn't like to be with them. Who is going to follow and respect a leader they feel doesn't like them?

It's the same thing when you enter the room with your mentee. Kids can tell from a mile away if you want to be with them or not. Does your face say, "I want to be here! I am so happy to be spending time with you!" Or does it say, "This is the last place I want to be. You are a waste of my time." Or does it say, "I'm preoccupied and watching the clock because I have a dozen other things to do." Actions truly do speak louder than words. Not only are we wired for joy and relationship, we are also wired to believe body language over what is said.

Jesus never made anyone feel like He didn't want to be with them. I bet He was engaged, made eye contact, and had a smile on His face.

He showed how much He loved those around him with His actions.

I never leave the presence of God feeling bad about myself. I always leave feeling loved and full of joy. Part of the gift of being a mentor is passing along the same joy we experience in our relationship with Jesus to the kids we love.

Heart of Compassion

My main prayer this past season has been for the Lord to give me a heart of compassion.

Many times throughout my week I am amazed at my lack of compassion, specifically toward children. There are certainly days when I don't look a thing like Jesus. I know I need to be consistently kind and compassionate, I just cannot do it for the life of me.

When I am frustrated with my son, I forget he is an innocent child with limited experience. On a daily basis, he is venturing into new territory and doing something he's never done before. I should celebrate such risk-taking, but instead, I get onto him because he didn't do it how I would do it.

The Bible says Jesus had compassion on the crowds because they were like sheep without a shepherd (Matthew 9:36). He didn't belittle them or get mad at their lack of progress. He met them where they were and cared for, taught, and guided them. When I picture Jesus doing this, I see Him smiling with peace in His eyes. He was never flustered or had somewhere else to be.

He surrounded Himself with the sick and outcast. He did whatever He could to enter into their world to make it a little bit better. I bet Jesus was a people magnet. Who wouldn't want to be around someone who truly cared for you and made you feel like the most important person alive?

As mentors, we can be like Jesus in this regard. When we listen to our mentee's story, allow the Lord to move our hearts as we put ourselves into his or her shoes. I want to remember the experiences each child endured because there is always a reason why they behave as they do.

When my mentee is an adult, I want him to look back and say, "I know without a doubt my mentor cared about me and wanted the best for me." And that's something we can only do through God's grace and with a heart of compassion.

Heart of Patience

Early in my mentoring journey, when I was trying to save every kid I mentored with my own efforts and giftings, I would get so frustrated when a kid didn't improve in a short period of time. In my pride I would say, "Well, this kid might be failing now, but just wait until I get a hold of him."

One day, I was having coffee with one of my mentors and venting my annoyance about a particular kid I had been mentoring for the past year. That's when my mentor turned to me and said, "Aren't you glad God doesn't get frustrated with us when we aren't perfect? It took a long time for this kid to get where he is today and it's probably going to take a long time for him to break out of that cycle. Just be patient with him."

I realized I was doing the exact opposite of Ephesians 4:2. I was not acting with humility and gentleness. Patience disappeared and I was certainly not tolerating him in love.

I am sure it could have been so easy for Jesus to give up on Judas. But instead, He washed his feet knowing hours later Judas would betray Him. He could have yelled at Peter, James, and John when they fell asleep in the Garden of Gethsemane. He could have said, "Just get your act together, Zacchaeus," or "What the heck, Martha? Stop cleaning and come hang out with Me!"

But He didn't. And He never gave up on me when I was up to my eyeballs in sin. He was constant and faithful even though I was not. Even today, some sin tendencies still rear their ugly heads. Jesus never shames me. He is patient.

Mentoring, just like becoming like Jesus, is a marathon not a sprint. We're in it for the long haul. Just because we don't see fruit right off doesn't mean fruit isn't growing. Sometimes what you say today won't actually register until years down the road. Let us follow Romans 8:25 and hope for what we don't see and wait for it with patience.

. . .

Heart of Faith

Look at all the major Bible characters and the faith they had. Noah had the faith to build a huge boat when there was no rain in the forecast. Moses led his people out of Egypt and had to cross the Red Sea. David faced Goliath as a teenager. Joseph endured betrayal, slavery, and prison before rising to royalty in Egypt. Without faith, it is impossible to please God.

Junior was an absolute handful. He gave our staff a run for their money each day with his antics. He was the smartest kid in the room, but you couldn't tell that by looking at his report card. He was a bona-fide leader, but he was leading in the wrong direction. He was the hardest fifth grader I've ever had to deal with. There were days I wanted to kick him out of our program because of his behavior. But our program staff and his mentor continued to love him. Day after day, year after year, we faithfully continued to pursue Junior.

Fast forward five years and Junior is entering his final years of high school. He is an outstanding young man, polite, respectful, and a joy to be around. He is still a leader and learning how to lead in the right direction. At summer camp last year, he won the award for best male camper.

This is one example of why I have to remember to have faith in the Lord no matter the situation. He is in control and He will transform a life at the right time. Our job is to have faith He will do exactly that.

The definition of faith is complete trust of confidence in someone or something. This makes me ask myself three questions:

- Do I have complete faith God can transform this kid's life?
- Do I have total faith that God can use this kid to positively impact the world?
- Do I have faith and believe God truly is who He says He is?

We maintain a heart of faith by staying near the presence of God. This is also why it is so important to stay in the Word and be surrounded by an encouraging community. They remind us that as we remain faithful to the Lord, He is faithful to turn a generational curse into a generational blessing.

One must have faith to venture into the life of an unknown kid, sacrificing your time, love, and energy to partner with the Lord as He moves in the heart of this child. We pray in faith for our mentee and believe he or she will receive breakthrough because we have faith. For faith is the assurance of things hoped for, the conviction of things not seen (Hebrews 11:1). Though we might not see the Lord moving in obvious ways, we can have faith and hope that He will never fail us.

Heart of Perseverance

Perseverance means doing something despite difficulty or delay in achieving success. If that doesn't sound like mentoring, I don't know what does. Any relationship will experience challenges if you stick with it long enough. This is even more the case when you build relationships with kids from hard places. There will be times when we must persevere, and when we do, we have an opportunity to really witness God's miraculous work.

Persevering in mentoring has two benefits. First, we have a front row seat to see miracles, life-transformation, and heart change. We get to experience God and His heart for His people in a whole new way.

Kevin never knew his father and his mom couldn't take care of him for various reasons. Since he was twelve, he lived with different members of the community, only seeing his family every once in a while. It seemed like everything in Kevin's life was stacked against him. He had every reason to give up and quit. But the Lord has had His hand on Kevin's life.

In high school, Kevin excelled athletically, academically, and socially. He had his mishaps every so often, but for the most part, Kevin has been a model citizen. After high school, Kevin decided to join the Marines. Kevin was dealt about as bad a hand as I've ever seen, but he has persistently overcome every obstacle with a smile. I got to witness the Lord protect Kevin and truly transform his life. Through Kevin, the Lord showed me any obstacle can be overcome with persistence.

The second benefit to perseverance is the transformation that happens in your life. There is no way I would be who I am today if I hadn't persisted in the journey of being a mentor. It has helped me grow in character and mature more than I ever could have imagined. It has been the joy of my life to invest in kids. But it hasn't been easy.

Mentoring kids who come from troubled situations has produced some sufferings in my life. But those sufferings produce perseverance; perseverance, character; and character, hope. And hope does not put us to shame, because God's love has been poured out into our hearts through the Holy Spirit, who has been given to us. Let us not grow weary of doing good, for in due season we will reap, if we do not give up (Romans 5:3-5).

Heart of Thanksgiving

Something happens to your heart when you focus on giving thanks for your mentee and for the relationship you have with him or her. Thanksgiving will completely transform your perspective toward your mentee.

Thanksgiving and disappointment are like oil and water. They do not mix. Thanksgiving also can't be in the same room with complaining, frustration, and anger. I know at first it can seem like there isn't a lot to be thankful for, especially if your kid is having a hard time. But I bet you can come up with some things to be grateful for.

Expressing gratitude to the Lord and to your mentee will always be beneficial. You can thank your mentee for hanging out with you. He doesn't have to choose to spend time with you or share his life with you. I have found shock and awe is the result when you thank your mentee for hanging out with you. Not only does it help your mentee feel valuable, but it sets an example for her to follow. The next time she shares something important to her, tell her thanks. When he makes an extra effort, tell him you're thankful he went the extra mile.

Rejoice always. Pray constantly. Give thanks in everything, for this is God's will for you in Christ Jesus—especially in your mentoring relationship (1 Thessalonians 5:16-18).

***

What an opportunity we have as mentors to be examples of Jesus Christ to our mentees. We can be a person who laughs easily and often with them, someone who will listen to their issues and cry along-side them. We can be someone who will patiently endure the ups and downs of a life and relationship. We believe our mentee is a world-changer and a history-maker. We persevere when most would give up. We are quick to enter into thanksgiving and praise, even when things don't go as planned.

This is the kind of mentor our kids need. This is the kind of mentor our kids deserve.

CHAPTER EIGHT

The Needs of a Mentee

THE LORD WAS onto something when He said, "It is not good for man to be alone" (Genesis 2:18). All of us need each other. Society has tricked our youth into believing we all need a big screen TV, a fancy car, or the newest pair of shoes—but those things aren't really needs at all.

My wife and I have a young daughter named Joanna who is the light of our lives. Joanna has two older brothers so, being our only girl, she gets just about anything she wants. When she was born, we went all out. We bought Joanna dresses, baby dolls, and a toy kitchen set. We got her everything a little girl could want. But do you know what Joanna really wants? She just wants to be loved. She wants our attention and she wants to laugh with us. Her desire is for smiles and eye contact, not dolls and toys.

The love a child needs can only be provided through a relationship with another human being. That's why we say relationships change lives. According to Maslow's Hierarchy of Needs, a child must first have their basic needs met in a safe and loving environment before they start to feel good about themselves and capable of fulfilling their full potential.

That explains the story of my friend Nigel. I met Nigel when I spent a few weeks in the small town of Pemba, Mozambique. Nigel and I became fast friends. Frankly, it's hard for anyone not to like Nigel. He's one of the kindest people I've ever come across. Nigel was a supervisor at the orphanage where we were working and was going to school at night to finish his college degree. He was an impressive young man.

One night, I asked to hear Nigel's story. He said, "It's quite simple, actually. We were poor—very poor. Lived in a small house and ate only rice and beans. But my mom and my dad loved us well. They taught us right from wrong and helped us believe we could do anything we put our minds to. And that is why I am here today."

Nigel didn't have a big house, the newest gaming system, or access to private sports training. But he did have love. And that gave him all he needed to become all he could be.

Many of the kids we mentor feel a love deficit. They simply aren't getting their relational needs met. For kids who don't have adults in their lives filling up their love tank, they believe the lies that they don't matter, can't do it, and are a failure. This leads to feelings of hurt, anger, fear, and shame and manifests in behaviors such as acting out, rebellion, perfectionism, or manipulation.

God created our mentees with relational needs. And we as mentors can meet these needs. Here are three ways we can show our mentees love in three unique ways:

Attention

Attention is a natural human need we all have. We have an innate need to be connected and known. When you receive attention, you feel valued. Attention deeply impacts your identity as it shows you that you matter. When someone spends time with you over work, hobbies, or other obligations, it communicates that you are the most important thing to them right now.

When we feel like nobody sees or hears us, when we feel alone and unknown, we become convinced we are not important or don't have value.

All throughout my junior high years, my coaches gave me attention. I don't even know if they were believers or if they were being intentional, but because they took time to notice a kid who was really hurting made a significant difference in my life. The attention they gave me helped me have the strength to make it day after day. The attention they gave me made me feel important, if only for a moment.

In a perfect world, the need for attention is met through a healthy, loving family. When emotional needs cannot be met in a family setting, kids will take matters into their own hands and figure out a way to get these needs met. When a child is seeking attention, they are seeking relationship. Bad behaviors, positive or negative, mean they are seeking relationship.

Where we look for attention is often developed as a child. My son, Stephen, really craves my attention. At least a few times a day, I hear, "Daddy, watch me, watch me!" as he jumps off the couch or throws a ball on the roof. He wants to know I care and he's worth caring about. That's why he calls my name. He wants his needs met in a positive way.

There have been times, however, I am not able to meet Stephen's need for attention. When that happens, he does whatever he has to do to get it. Whether it is screaming at me or throwing a ball at my head, he will do whatever he has to do to get my attention. One way or another, he is going to get that need met.

When the kids we mentor aren't getting their need for attention and relationship met, they will do whatever they have to do to get their needs met.

Negative Attention

Your mentee may be looking for, or even demanding attention through the following behaviors:

Class Clown

Some mentees get their need for attention met by acting out and becoming the class clown. Sure, it might make the teacher angry, but it gets 30 sets of eyes looking at them. That feeling is well worth detention or spending the day suspended.

. . .

Dressing or Acting Outlandishly

If you consider yourself a sports fan in the least bit, you know Denis Rodman is a basketball player in the 90s who was famous for dying his hair odd colors and dressing up in the most absurd outfits. If you hear Denis's story of how he grew up, it makes a lot of sense why he would dress that way. He never got attention, and this is how he made up for it. For our mentees, dying their hair, getting crazy haircuts, and wearing quirky outfits is a surefire way to get people to pay attention to them, even if it's a passing glance.

Being the "Tough Guy"

If a child gets into a fight, people will be talking about it and waiting for him or her to start a fight again. If the child wins the fight, he or she might even get some respect out of it from their peers as well. This was me in high school. I worked out a ton so I could have huge muscles and get attention. I wanted to look like a manly man. I said a bunch of cuss words. I threatened to beat people up (thank God no one took me up on the challenge because I was terrified inside). I disrespected authority so everyone knew no one could tell me what to do. And all because I wanted people to look at me.

I've seen this in girls as well. Intimidation, bullying, and gossip can be used as major tools to get people to pay attention to you. When you are seen as the "mean girl" or leader of any clique, you are getting attention. And for some of our girls, attention is enough of a motivator to continue these behaviors.

Throwing a Fit

Screaming, yelling, kicking, punching (even pretending to), slamming doors, or throwing things is another way children get attention. Typically these behaviors appear in our younger mentees, but it can also happen with teenagers as well. Their actions are saying, "If you won't pay attention to me, I'm going to cause such a scene that you have to look my way. It will be worth it even if I have to face consequences."

Doing Whatever They Have to Do to Fit In

Sometimes, especially as they get older, our mentees will change behaviors or interests depending on the crowd they are trying to join. This is why you might see your mentee being an athlete one year, a musician the next, and a pothead the year after. Like a chameleon, they transform themselves depending on their surroundings simply to get noticed by their peers. You can also see this when teens are one way with their family, another way at school, and yet another way with their friends.

Drugs and Alcohol

I was in junior high and we stole some beer from my friend's dad. We waited until midnight, snuck out of the house, and went in the alley to crack open our first cold one. As me and my friends sat there, acting cool and feeling grown up, I remember thinking beer was the worst drink I ever tasted. But I finished the beer and drank another. Why? To look cool and to get my friend's attention. The same thing happened with cigarettes. It was a terrible experience, but I continued to do it because I wanted friends and this was what I thought it took to get people to hang out with me.

Sexual Activity

Like bugs to a light on a dark summer's night, teenage boys gather around the guy who can tell the story about rounding third base last Friday night. So many boys use woman and sex to get attention from their friends. They want so badly to be seen as cool and macho, so they use their sexual activities to impress others.

This isn't just seen with boys. Especially today, with a culture infatuated with sex, many teenaged girls often think being sexy is the only way guys will notice them. Attention from a guy who only wants you for physical purposes is still attention. Dressing provocatively and making oneself look as sexy as possible, especially via social media, is a surefire way for some girls to get boys to look their way.

These are just a few ways our mentees might try to get attention in negative ways. Most of the time, our mentees don't like doing these negative behaviors. But they care more about getting their emotional needs met than the consequences which come with these behaviors. Our kids aren't bad kids. They are just trying to take care of themselves. We call this the "need behind the deed."

Positive Attention

Sometimes our mentees seek getting their attention needs met by doing positive things—behaviors which appear good and acceptable, but at the root are simply seeking attention.

The Perfect One

Some of our kids believe they have to act perfect, be perfect, do perfect work, in order to get anyone to pay attention to them. They strive and push themselves to earn someone's love through their actions. Making straight A's and excelling in sports are both great things, but they may be doing the right things for the wrong reasons. While on the outside, all looks good, decipher the root motive. What is the need behind the deed?

The Easy One

I've seen this play out a lot, especially in children who have older siblings with strong personalities. They think the best way to get attention is to go along with the flow. Their mindset is, "If I can just not rock the boat and make life easier for my parents and this household, I will get praise for that. It doesn't matter what I really want to do. What matters is only making choices that will get the most people to give me the most attention.

The Parent Pleaser

I have seen many kids participate in an activity because it is what their mom or dad wants them to do. You see this in the son who plays football only because his dad wants him to be the next football all-star, or the daughter who is a cheerleader because her mom wants her to be on the cheer squad. Theses kids may take specific classes, join certain clubs, and even pick their college major or career all because they want their parent to be proud of them. They sacrifice their dreams for the positive attention of their mom or dad.

The Award Winner

The more awards the child wins, the more positive attention the parent, teacher, or coach gives to them. When I gave out awards as a junior high coach at the end of each season, I was always amazed at how much the certificates meant to a kid. To me, it was a piece of paper. To them, it was a ticket to receive praise from their parents.

The Teacher's Pet

Is your mentee always the first one to volunteer to help out? Are they the ones willing to come early and stay late? As a teacher, I always had a few kids who would stick around after practice to help me clean up. They would do the hardest jobs with a smile on their face because they liked the attention they received when helping.

***

Jesus and Attention

Jesus spent most of His time with people who needed Him the most—the outcast, the poor, the sick, and those who society rejected. He didn't give them a handbook or resources or training. He gave them His presence. And a relationship with Jesus changed everything.

Take the story of Zacchaeus. Here was this little dude who no one liked. He was rich, dishonest, and unpopular. But Jesus spotted him up in a tree and said, "Zacchaeus, I'm coming over to your house for dinner tonight." Jesus pursued Zacchaeus when no one else would. He did this because the "Son of man came to seek and save the lost" (Luke 19:1-10). Jesus gave Zacchaeus His attention, which showed he had value. And that alone brought salvation to Zacchaeus's house.

Attention and Self-Esteem

A child's first relationships are extremely important in helping them establish a sense of value for themselves. If a child grows up thinking no one wants to be with them, then it is easy for the enemy to lie and tell them they are worthless. This can have major implications on their self-esteem, self-value, and self-confidence.

One of our mentors, Thomas, was dropping off Derek at his apartment complex. As Thomas pulled up to Derek's unit, he said, "Hey man, when you get to the door, open it and wave to me so I know you made it in safely. Cool?"

This took Derek by surprise, as no one had ever done that for him before.

"Why do I need to do that?" asked Derek.

"Well, because I care about you and I want you to be safe."

Derek shrugged and got out of the car. He then stopped, turned around. "Thanks for making sure I'm okay," he said, and walked into his apartment.

His face said it all. It finally clicked that Thomas cared about Derek and showed his love by being there.

Doing things like showing up to events, making eye contact, and just being there for our mentees when they least expect it speaks value and worth. It can change how a kid sees themselves and could change his or her life.

***

Another need mentees have is acceptance—to be truly loved and accepted for who they are, not what they do. Being accepted with unconditional love is hard to find in our performance-based culture, but it is something all children need in order to fulfill their potential.

Acceptance

I walked in the door of a brand new discipleship training school in Nashville, Tennessee and noticed a line in the hallway. "What's going on? Why are we all crammed in this hallway?" That's when I learned we were in line to meet Don Finto.

I could tell there was something different about this man. In his mid-eighties, he was the epitome of joy. His smile was radiant and his laughter filled the air. When I got to the front of the line, Don grabbed my face, got on his tip-toes and kissed me on the cheek. Then he turned my head and kissed me on the other cheek. I was totally fazed by what just happened. Don then gave me what felt like 15-minute bear hug while he laughed in my ear. As he was hugging me, he just kept saying "I love you. I love you. I love you."

I had never been so uncomfortable in my life. I had never been so embarrassed in my life. I had also never been so accepted in my whole life.

Don and I still laugh about that moment today. I know it paints a funny picture, but there is nothing funny about the impact his acceptance had in my life. If I stop to think on that moment, I am overwhelmed with emotion and thanksgiving. Don gave me the acceptance I had longed for. I have grown to yearn for the hug and kiss of Don. He knows this, too, because every time he is with me he gives me the acceptance only a father can give.

When trauma or brokenness attacks a family, the enemy uses this opportunity to make a child feel insignificant and rejected. To make matters worse, these feelings can also materialize in friendships and social interactions. It's one thing to not be accepted by your family, but it's double the impact when you're not accepted by your peers as well.

An unfortunate event happen to me in sixth grade when all, and I mean all, of my friends turned on me because they thought I was homosexual. Those rumors lasted into middle school and I had a really hard time making friends because of it. It did major damage to how I saw myself. When my parents got divorced when I was in eighth grade, it all seemed to pile up.

My need to be accepted was at an all-time high. I would do anything to be accepted into a group. I was the kid at the party who would do whatever the cool kids told him to do. The fear of rejection has haunted me my whole life and one of the main ways it showed up was through performance-based love.

From an early age, I felt I had to performed to earn love. I believed I had to earn love. If I can't be accepted by a man who I can see, how can I feel accepted by a God I cannot see? This affected every part of my life from friendships to my spiritual life. It started as a teenager, but it rose to the surface during my mid-twenties.

It showed up in my first serious romantic relationship. I was dating an amazing girl from a great family. It was a great relationship, except for one issue: I did whatever I could to earn her love. Keep in mind I had no clue I was doing this—it was all subconscious. I was the best boyfriend, but with selfish motives. I believed if I bought her enough flowers, took her on the best dates, and did whatever she wanted me to do, then she would love me and accept me.

When things didn't work out, I was absolutely crushed. How could she break up with me when I treated her perfectly? Only now do I see how that thought process was a huge part of the problem. I wasn't selflessly loving her, but the opposite. It was the idea of being accepted through love I was pursuing, not her.

I share this to show how powerful and long-lasting is the need to be accepted. If this happened to me in my mid-twenties, after I had matured a little and gone through some counseling and healing, think how a teenager might feel?

It's no wonder there are over 700,000 teenagers in gangs today. Gangs target vulnerable teens who are trying to fit in and be accepted. The number one reason they join a gang is to feel accepted. They just want to belong. When kids are loved only for what they do, one of two things develop: a mindset founded on striving and perfectionism to earn love, or a mindset founded on apathy and lack of trying because they believe they are worthless.

Our children will find acceptance somewhere, make no mistake about it. We as mentors have the opportunity to make sure they find acceptance in a positive way. Here are some questions I hear often from mentors when talking about accepting our mentees just as they are:

How do you communicate acceptance to a mentee when he is making poor choices?

- Keep pursuing and being present. You presence alone speaks to your acceptance.
- You can love the person and not love his actions, but you

have to say it out loud. "Look, I love you and I care a ton about you. I am not going anywhere and I'm in your corner, but let's talk about your actions."

How do I give my mentee acceptance while showing where they can grow and change? Is that even possible?

- Do not lower the bar of what is acceptable behaviors. Acceptance does not mean you believe they have no room to grow, or they've fulfilled their potential.
- Be very careful when giving correction as a mentor. We are not their parents. But when we do correct, give healthy re-direction while re-affirming who they are and we are for them. Affirm and accept who they are while not allowing negative behaviors to continue.
- Acceptance is being there for your mentee with or without their reciprocation.

How does acceptance counteract the lies the enemy speaks in the midst of disappointment and failure?

- When a child fails or is disappointed, it is a golden opportunity to reinforce our acceptance of them as a person despite the situation.
- Remind the child your love is not based on performance, and neither is God's love for him or her.

What are some practical ways we can communicate acceptance to our mentees?

- Be careful what you say and how you say it. Our children are always listening to and picking up on our feelings and attitudes. They're listening to how we speak to them, about them, and closely watching how we react to other people.
- Whenever we have a strong, negative reaction to our child's behavior, it is wise to ask ourselves what is really going on. What are you really reacting to? What do you fear will hap-

pen here? Address your own feelings in order to effectively empathize with your mentee. If we don't, we risk communicating we don't accept them just as they are.

- Learn to demonstrate acceptance by speaking your acceptance over them. Don't keep acceptance as merely how you feel in your heart toward your mentee.

As we show acceptance, our mentees will learn how to accept others as well. Their receiving graced-based love will teach them to give grace-based love. The temptation is to think that speaking intentional phrases of encouragement may be weird or awkward. But the truth is, our kids need to hear it.

Even in the hard times, I pray God gives you the endurance and encouragement to have the same attitude toward your mentee that Christ Jesus has toward you and him or her. When we accept one another as Christ accepts us, this brings God glory and praise.

Affirmation

Affirmation says, "You have what it takes to succeed and I believe in you."

Our kids need to be affirmed. They need to know they have what it takes to be successful. If they don't hear it from a caring adult, they will hear the opposite from the enemy. The enemy tells our kids they are not enough. Affirmation encourages our kids to pursue all the Lord has for them. We get to look our kids in the eyes and say, "You can do it. I believe in you. You are enough." This shows them it is healthy to take risks and challenge themselves. This fills them with self-confidence and a positive identity.

Our kids want to be affirmed. They want to know others see that they have what it takes to be successful.

My mentor, Steve, was the most encouraging guy I'd ever met. Even though his direct words made me a little uncomfortable at first, I started looking for ways to be with him. He was intentional in texting or calling me to share who the Lord thought I was. As our relationship was established, his words of affirmation changed.

When Steve sensed I was hungry for more, he started asking more direct questions about situations in my life. Such as, "How do you feel about your father?" I'd give my answer. Then he'd say, "What does the Lord have to say about that?" And I'd answer. He'd say, "If how you feel and what the Lord feels do not line up, what are you going to do about that?" He helped me process an action plan. Then he would say, "Can I encourage you in this and hold you accountable to take action in this area?" I'd say yes. And he did. And all along the way he'd affirm I was "a mighty man of God" and I had what it took to become godly in this area of my life.

Steve's words built me into the man I am today and offered security in the following areas of my life:

- I didn't know I had what it took to be a man.
- I had no idea how to steward my emotions.
- I didn't know I had something to offer.
- I didn't know what my strengths were.
- I didn't know God had a plan and purpose for my life.
- I didn't feel loved.

But Steve's affirmation gave me the confidence to:

- Deal with my anger through counseling
- Forgive my father and deal with the trauma of my childhood
- Seek out how to truly follow God with all of my heart
- Find my purpose in life
- Grow up, mature, and learn how to be a Godly husband and father
- Actually believe I'm a man of God and grow in self-worth and self-confidence

Words of affirmation are the weapons which fight against the lies of the enemy and the lies of this world. A lack of affirmation creates a void. Every child has room to grow. Encouragement helps them to grow in specific areas. What you encourage in them will naturally flourish. A lack of affirmation isn't necessarily experienced as disapproval, though it may be.

Affirmation tells you who you are and who you are not. It is the ultimate call-up when a mentor says, "You are a man of God," or "You're better than how you're acting right now."

When I was single, I played in as many as three basketball leagues at the same time. One was a local church league. As a cocky and massive 25 year old, I loved this league. I had no issue dunking on any old man who got in my way, even Pastor Joe and Elder Bob. I also had no problem screaming at the referees if I felt like he missed a call.

One game, my team was playing a team made up of older gentlemen who were accomplished professionals here in Dallas. They were just here to have a good time. I was going up against Nick, a best friend of my girlfriend's father. We had met a few times and Nick was a respected man of God in the community.

By halftime, the score was out of hand and the game was almost over, but I was still giving it to the refs. I complained. I yelled. I pouted. I had been having a great game, but I still wanted more. My arrogance and pride was getting out of hand. As the game was coming to an end, I went up for a dunk. A member of the other team barely touched my arm and I missed the shot. I raised my hands and screamed, "C'mon, Ref!"

Nick grabbed both of my shoulders and made me face him. I was bigger than Nick, but his dad-strength came out at that moment. He looked me right in my eyes and said, "Zach. Stop it. That's not who you are!"

He could have chewed me out—he had every right to. But instead, Nick spoke identity into me. He spoke promise and life over me and my future. Nick called me up instead of calling me out. And that made a huge impact on who I am today.

All of us need affirmation to some degree. Even Jesus needed it.

Just as Jesus came out of the water after being baptized by John the Baptist, God affirms Him from heaven saying, "You are my beloved Son; with you I am well pleased." Here, God affirms Jesus before He starts His ministry (Matthew 3:13-17). Jesus is affirmed of who He is, not what He does. God says, "You are my son" which gives Jesus identity. God says, "With you I am well pleased" which gives Jesus self-worth.

Right after He was baptized, Jesus was sent out into the wilderness for forty days to be tempted by the devil (Matthew 4:1-11). But God's affirmation of Jesus's identity gave Him what He needed to endure this hard time. I believe these words of affirmation gave Jesus everything He needed to start His ministry and leave the world a different place.

If Jesus needs affirmation, how much more do we?

Dreaming For Your Mentee

Sometimes we as mentors have to dream for our mentees because they don't always have the ability to dream for themselves. They simply don't know what is out there.

I became a teacher because it was either retail, teacher, or doctor. Those were really the only three professions I knew about. I went to the college I did because it was the only college an adult told me about. I thought all colleges were the same. It wasn't until later I learned different colleges specialize in different areas of education.

Someone in college said they majored in business and I had no idea what they were talking about. Marketing, finance, entrepreneur—what was all of that? We have a saying that "You can't be what you can't see."

As a mentor, you get the opportunity to speak the future of your mentee into existence. Call out the good things you see for them. You can spark visions for their future with words like:

- "You know, you're a good leader. I bet you would make a great coach or CEO one day."
- "You really seem to enjoy taking chances and can withstand failure and learn from it. I bet you could start your own business one day."
- "You have a heart to help people. Have you ever thought about going into health care as a nurse or therapist?"
- "I notice you have an ear for music. Is there an instrument you'd like to learn to play?"
- "You are very artistic. Have you ever thought about using your art as a career?"
- "I see you solve puzzles and find solutions very easily. Let's research some engineering careers that might interest you."

Every child is different. Each has different skills, dreams, and desires. The best way to give a mentee love is through attention, affirmation, and the opportunity to dream.

CHAPTER NINE

The Mentee's Family

TIMMY WAS A new kid in our afterschool mentoring program. He was in our program about a week when he started to stand out due to his negative behavior. Our staff was shocked when Timmy, an eight-year-old, talked about how "real men have sex with as many women as possible and fight whenever someone disrespects them." We had dealt with inappropriate comments every now and then, but this was next level.

The day I met Timmy's mom, Janet, was the moment when I realized how important the mentee's family is in a mentoring relationship. We called Janet and explained what her son was saying. Her response, "Well, that's what real men do. That's what I'm teaching him."

While most of the parents and guardians in our organization see eye-to-eye regarding what is best for their child, some do not. It is really hard to mentor a kid when your guidance is the opposite of what his or her family is teaching. After all, who is a kid going to believe—their family member or you, a new mentor who they barely knows?

A common thread in a mentor/mentee relationship that isn't flourishing is often a disconnect between the mentor and the mentee's family. Not only is the family—in particular the mother if your mentee lives in a father-absent home—the gatekeeper to your mentee, but they are the most influential people in the life of your mentee. It is vital you get to know the family, partner with the family, and honor the family as you invest in their son or daughter.

Mentally placing myself in the places of the parent or guardian has helped me better invest in my mentee's family. Would I want my son or daughter's mentor to say hi to me? Would I feel comfortable allowing my child to spend time with a stranger without first getting to know me? How do I know I can trust them? What are the key things I'd want to know about someone before they visit and interact with my child?

When the family of your mentee flourishes, your mentee flourishes. When they struggle, it rubs off on the mentee. If you really want the best for your mentee, to include the family and do whatever you can to help them succeed as well.

Here are some important things to keep in mind as you invest in the most important people in your mentee's life.

Meeting the Family: Let's all get on the same page!

It takes more than a commitment on your end to have a successful mentoring relationship. Your mentee and their parent/guardian have to be on board for the relationship. Even better is inviting your family along in the process as well. Mentoring relationships that start with a commitment in the beginning are more likely to last long term.

For these three parties (mentor and family, mentee, parent/guardian), setting ground rules on the front end is a must. Clarify what is a mentor's goal and what a mentor does. Here's an outline of how you can answer those questions in a conversation with everyone in the same room.

- What is a mentor's main goal? To build a relationship with you.
  - A mentor helps you feel safe
  - A mentor and mentee have fun together
  - A mentor asks you questions and helps you grow
- How do they do that? The Three A's
  - *Attention:* When you see this guy, you know he is there to see you. You will get to hangout, play, talk, eat meals, share stories. If you play sports he will come to your

games. If you play an instrument, he'll come to your concerts.

- *Affirmation:* When you hang out together, this gal is going to encourage you and speak truth. Your mentor will celebrate you and cheer you on as you grow.
- *Acceptance:* When you mess up, his job is to help you no matter what. He will encourage you and help you see areas where you're growing. He will celebrate you because of you, not because of what you do. When you're accepted no matter what, you will feel loved, secure, and that you belong.

After explaining what a mentor's job is, it's great to give everyone a chance to share a part of their story to get to know each other. For example,

- Mentor shares their background, interests, and answers any questions the mentee and guardian have.
- Mentee shares their background, interests, and answers the mentor's questions.
- Parent/Guardian can share anything she'd like to say about her son and their background.

Once you as the mentor explain what mentoring is, and share stories, it's time to make a commitment. Here are things each person should commit to in order to foster a successful mentor relationship:

Mentor Commitments:

- Communication: Mentor will initiate, communicate, and be a man or woman of his/her word to mentee and parent/guardian.
- Time: Mentor will make plans to invest consistent time with their mentee.
- Character: Mentor commits to growing in character and speaking truth into his or her mentee. Mentor will pray for the mentoring relationship on a regular basis.

- Safety: Mentor will report how the relationship is going to parent/guardian in a transparent manner on a regular basis.

Mentee Commitments:

- Communication: Mentee will respond to Mentor's communication in a timely manner.
- Time: Mentee will make time to spend with their mentor.
- Character: Mentee will be willing to grow.
- Safety: Mentee will report how the relationship is going to parent/guardian in a transparent manner on a regular basis.

Parent/Guardian Commitment:

- Communication: Parent/Guardian will communicate regularly with mentor.
- Time: Parent/Guardian will invite the mentor into the child's life by making time for the mentor relationship to happen.
- Character: Parent/Guardian will pray for the mentoring relationship on a regular basis.
- Safety: Parent/Guardian will report and share feedback about the mentoring relationship to help it grow and stay healthy.

Having this conversation at the beginning of the relationship will help give everyone a clear vision for the relationship, but it doesn't stop there. How will you plan to enforce and track your commitments to one another? Who will hold you accountable? Mentoring organizations exist to help administrate this part of the mentoring relationship. We highly encourage mentoring within a community/organization to ensure the health and safety of your mentor relationship.

Meeting your mentee for the first time can be a pretty intimidating event for all parties, but it doesn't have to be. Here are a couple things to remember:

- **Pray.** Cover this meeting in prayer. Ask for the Lord to give you favor and to break down any walls or lies that might be in the heart of your mentee. Ask your friends and family to cover the interaction as well.

- **It's okay to be nervous!** Yes, he or she is only a kid, but first impressions are a big deal. Just be you. Smile, make eye contact, and ask questions. You have what it takes to be a loving mentor. God qualifies the called instead of calls the qualified. Believe that.
- **You don't have to put on a show.** Please don't believe you have to be anyone other than yourself. Remember, your mentee isn't looking for someone to entertain him; he is looking for someone to show up and love him no matter what.
- **Be like Jesus!** Smile. Laugh. Ask her questions about herself and interests. Talk about yourself. Be sure to give a high five, fist bump, or pat on the back. Let him or her know you are glad to be there.
- **This is only the beginning.** Don't worry if the conversation is short or one-sided or awkward. This happens. Making conversation with an elementary or junior high kid is hard. It's only going to get better. To encourage more dialogue, try to ask open-ended questions, ones that don't require the one-word answer of "yes" or "no."
- **Don't read too much into it!** Give your mentee the benefit on the doubt. For example, if he's not talkative, maybe he's nervous. Maybe he's shy. Maybe he's having a bad day. Don't let the enemy speak lies to you such as, "you're not cool enough" or "he doesn't like you." Believe the best.

As you meet your mentee, try your best to remember important things about him or her and to be encouraging. Speak truth and help him or her feel like the most important kid in the world to you. Pretty simple stuff. No need to over-complicate it.

Importance of Their Family

The most important person in your mentee's life is their parent/guardian. Mentors value the mentee's family by:

- Communicating regularly

- Always give as much information about activities and scheduled events as possible to their parent/guardian
- Expressing thankfulness for being trusted to be a part of their child's life
- Looking for opportunities to love and serve the family
- Praying for them

The United States Department of Education says one of the most significant indicators of a successful mentor relationship is parental involvement. Every mentor should be challenged by that statement. Want this mentor relationship to be as successful as possible? Find ways to build relationship with their family as well.

When I started mentoring Zay, he lived on the second floor of an apartment complex. The parking lot in front of his building was always full. Every time I came to pick him up for a dinner, I had this temptation to just text him when I was outside so he could run out to me. But it occurred to me this was an opportunity to have two in-person moments with his mom every time I saw him. I made it my intention to use those times, even if it was just for two minutes, to connect and build a relationship with his mom.

At the same time, my wife was considering ways she could build a relationship with Zay's mom as well. She and her friends had just finished reading a book called *Be the Bridge* by Latasha Morrison. They were contemplating what it would look like to start a small group to talk about racial reconciliation. Zay's mom immediately came to mind. "I need to invite Kyra to lead this with me," my wife said.

Now, consider this: a white woman inviting a black woman into a small group to lead a bunch of white women. Does that sound like the easiest invitation to make or respond to? Well, it worked. Kyra shared it was uncomfortable at times. But as the women continued to meet, Kyra was intrigued to see this group of white women dealing with their prejudices, doing their homework, and asking for her feedback and perspective as a black woman. This invitation, and the commitment I made to seize the small opportunities to interact with a mom at the front door has helped forge a lifelong relationship between our two families.

Honoring Dad: Honor above all

If your mentee has a father who is not present, tread lightly on this sensitive issue. No matter what a mentee's dad has done, he is still the child's father. There will always be a paternal connection between a child and father. When you are with your mentee, honor the father in all you say.

When you do discuss the father, do not attack his character or actions. You can address the child's feelings and affirm the feelings have validity. Be more of a listener than anything when a child is processing this hurt. A good phrase to use is, "I'd be upset/mad/hurt/sad too if my father did that. I'm sorry and I'm here for you."

If a child's father does enter the picture, honor him by communicating from time to time with him and partnering with him as best you can. The goal is reconciliation and restoration. Do everything you can to make it safely happen if the opportunity presents itself.

We had the opportunity to sit down with the father of a young man who is in our mentoring program. The dad was curious about us and what we did. He also felt a little attacked that his son needed a mentor and he wanted to get to know the men who were investing in his kid.

As we sat down with the dad, we explained who we are and our intentions to help his son become all the Lord intended for him. We told the dad we wanted to work alongside him to create the best environment for his son to grow up well. Here's what he said:

> "I never knew my father, never even saw a picture. That was always hard for me to deal with. And the statistics you hear about kids without dads are real. I was one of them. I got involved in the wrong crowd, did drugs, went to prison... when you don't have a father figure in your life it's easy to go the wrong way.
>
> It's hard being separated and having to split time with my son's mom, but I know I have to make it work. I have other kids with my first ex, and it's hard. She died a year and a half ago in a car wreck, and now my daughters stay with their grandmother on her side. I'm hoping to work it out where they can be with me, but it's not an option right now. At least I get my son every other week.

I'm thankful my son is a part of your organization and that he has mentors who love God. If I'm honest, I don't have a real relationship with God. I know that's important but it's just not a priority for me right now. I want more for my son and I think you are giving him that."

When you do ministry in the name of Jesus, you can expect the Lord to open doors you never even knew existed. Here we are, a mentoring organization, getting to preach the Gospel to the absent-father of one of our mentees. Who knows what the Lord is going to do in his heart through us mentoring his son. The Lord is after the hearts of His people, and that not only means your mentee, but perhaps his family members as well.

***

When you signed up to mentor a child, you might not have had plans to get to know their family as well. My encouragement to you is to make your mentee's family a priority. Not only will it help your relationship with your mentee, it will show honor and value to the family. It is a great way to truly love your neighbor and get to know those who might be different than you. You never know what the Lord will do through your intentionality. How amazing would it be if your mentee's entire family came to know the Lord because of your actions? Pray for them and pursue them. Honor them and bless them. Generations can be changed all because you loved this family with the love of Jesus.

CHAPTER TEN

Practical Principles of Mentoring

WHEN I FIRST started mentoring, I remember having no idea what to do, what to say, or where to go. Not feeling equipped led to discouragement, and discouragement caused me to almost quit mentoring all together. I struggled with questions like:

- "Is what I'm doing even working?"
- "Are they even listening to me?"
- "Do they like spending time with me?"

The purpose of this chapter is to help equip and encourage you to stay in the mentoring relationship. It is meant to help give you tools needed to build the best relationship possible with your mentee.

As we've discussed already, the most important thing about mentoring is to love our mentees with the love of Jesus. Just showing up and being a caring, trusting adult can literally change the trajectory of a family line. However, there are some practical principals I have learned that could be helpful to you as a mentor. There are some things to keep in mind as you start or continue on in your mentoring journey. Most of these things I have learned from failing, so please learn from my mistakes and avoid them yourself.

Be Gentle: Do your kids experience Jesus when they talk to you?

My friend, Joel Busby, likes to compare dealing with people to cooking a steak for friends. He says, "Just like you think about who will be eating the steak when you prepare it, you must think about the heart of a person when you are talking to them. You prepare the steak in such a way that the person will eat it, enjoy it, and allow it to nourish them. In the same way, you must tell the truth in such a way the heart of the person will hear it and accept it." For example, if you give someone a rare steak when they asked for it well done, it's not going to go over well. If they like their steak seasoned with garlic, but instead you give them a hot dog, they're won't enjoy it. If they expect only to be served a dry, tough steak, but you instead cook it to perfection with butter and spices and add their favorite sides of mashed potatoes and roasted vegetables, it will be far better received and remembered.

For example, if your mentee is shy and lacks self-confidence, speaking bluntly and firmly might not be the best approach. However, it might be exactly what the brash, cocky athlete needs to hear. You prepare your words in such a way the person will hear it and it will nourish them.

I try to picture Jesus talking to my mentee. What would His tone be like? How would He phrase a question or shine a light on a destructive habit? After all, a soft answer turns away wrath, but a harsh word stirs up anger and a gentle tongue is a tree of life (Proverbs 15:1 and 4). When in doubt, think about the Fruit of the Spirit (Galatians 5:22-23). Follow the wisdom of the Holy Spirit and the example the Bible sets before you.

Don't Take Things Personally: Not taking things personally is a superpower

My friend Josh Meadows leads a ministry in North Carolina for kids from hard situations. He told me, "The worst thing you can do as a mentor is get offended." Kids will say some pretty harsh things. They will try to find your limit. Sooner or later, every mentor feels the temptation to get angry, feel resentful, and throw in the towel.

You will feel like your mentee does not appreciate what you're offering, that he fails to listen to your sage wisdom. There will be tangible evidence which leads you to believe you're in the right. These feelings are real. But here's the thing: you're mentoring a kid. Getting angry or disappointed in a kid's actions is like being mad because the ocean is still wet. When you feel those things rising in your heart, the best thing to do is step back, breathe, and remind yourself to trust the process. Don't take it personally.

Feeling discouraged about a kid's progress is one thing, but taking credit for their success is another. You may also feel tempted to attribute their success as your success. If they get an A in class, it's because of you. If they score a touchdown, it's because of you. If they show improvement, it must be because of your investment paying off. Beware! We cannot take credit for their success nor take their mistakes personally.

We cannot focus on the fruit. Mentors focus on the roots.

Listen More Than You Talk: Don't be the advice monster

Our friends at the 411 House in East Temple say it like this, "Don't give them life lessons. Give them life." Your words are important, but not more important than your presence and your listening. Mentoring is meant to be tailored to the mentee's needs. We may come into our mentor relationships with strengths, skills, gifts, and passions to impart. But good mentors intentionally call out, honor, and develop what their mentee already has. Mentors have the opportunity to empower their mentee to take steps in his personal development toward a path to success.

Mentoring is Access to Your Network: It's all about who you know, not what you know

Good mentors are networkers at heart. Mentors are an entry point into a network of trusted relationships and humble enough to know that connecting their mentee to more resources and relationships will leave them better off. Networking breaks off our pride and creates greater levels of trust.

I want to introduce my mentee to as many talented and diverse followers of Jesus as possible. This way, he will have a number of options of men to emulate. He will be exposed to different skills, perspectives, and ideas.

Instead of trying to answer all of your mentee's questions, who do you know who could provide a better and wiser answer? Who could give them greater access to something they're interested in? How could you use relationships to further verify what you've been trying to show them on your own? The people you connect your mentee to will strengthen their ability to trust, to improve their social skills, and grow as learners. Sharing your network will give your mentee an example to follow in the future when they will be networking with others.

How can you challenge your mentee to start networking? Who could you connect them with so they can grow?

Kids Learn More by Observing: More is Caught than Taught

Hebrews 1:1-2 says, "Long ago, at many times and in many ways, God spoke to our fathers by the prophets, but in these last days he has spoken to us by his Son, whom he appointed the heir of all things, through whom also he created the world" (ESV).

In Jesus, God gave us a living example. This is the greatest thing God could have ever done for us: We can see Him, relate to Him, be challenged by Him, and learn to follow Him because "The Word became flesh and dwelt among us..." (John 1:14). He gave us a front row seat to His life, death, and resurrection.

Mentoring is only as powerful as it is incarnational. We don't send texts with instructions on how to pray, how to mow the lawn, and how to love our moms. We pray together, mow the lawn together, and do the dishes after dinner together. We incarnate the truths with our time and presence. We personify the principles. We don't paint a picture of what it looks like to be a godly man. We are the picture.

Kids will always retain information differently based on their environment, their temperament, and cognitive ability. But every kid with a mentor has a significant advantage: they are experiencing a living message about what life is about.

Think back to someone who influenced you. Can you remember anything he actually said? Any one liners that changed your life? Chances are, there are only a few things you remember him saying. But you do remember what he did. You remember parts of his character you appreciated. You may not remember what he said, but you remember how he said it. Kids remember experiences, not words. They remember how you made them feel.

Mentors impart more than wisdom and knowledge. Mentors provide signposts for our character and spirit and attitudes to develop. They are relatable. They let you see the way they live. Mentors don't tell you how to do it, or give you a list of everything you did wrong—they show you how to do it. They fail alongside you. They give you feedback and encouragement.

The saying goes, "More is caught than taught." A mentee is going to learn a whole lot more by watching you be a positive and productive Jesus-follower than by you telling them how to be a positive and productive Jesus-follower. It's the Benjamin Franklin quote: "Tell me and I forget, teach me and I remember, involve me and I learn."

Our kids will learn how to be a spouse by watching you selflessly be a loving spouse. They will learn to pray by watching when you stop to pray, hearing you, and praying with you. They will forgive others because you showed them what it looks like to forgive those who have hurt you. Simply let them observe you.

One day, I was talking to my mentee on the phone and I mentioned I was on my way to the grocery store. He said, "Can I come?"

"You want to come to the grocery store with me? That doesn't sound fun."

He laughed. "Not like I have anything better to do. Come get me."

Mentoring doesn't have to be extravagant. It's all about being with your mentee. They don't want to be impressed; they just want you. So invite them over for dinner, take them to church, run errands with them, and let them play with you and your kids. Let your family get to know them and include them in the normal, everyday activities you already participate in. Mentoring can be a great family activity and way to serve the Lord together.

Give Positive Feedback: Feedback is an invitation to get better

Kids learn from the feedback they receive. It is a major part of their maturation process. When a mentor is added into this maturation process, they provide a significant source of feedback. No matter what a mentor does, their mentee will receive it as feedback. This is why we have to be prayerful and intentional with what we do, say, how we say it, and how frequently we say it. We have to package feedback in such a way the mentee will receive it in the best way possible.

I know a mentor who uses a phone app called MarcoPolo to video message with his mentee. He grabs a cup of coffee, sits down at his desk, and shoots his mentee a video. It may be a thought he had, or an encouragement he prepared, or an observation he had about something his mentee did. After he shares, he ends his videos with three words, "I love you."

The feedback he shares is always positive, thoughtful, and meaningful. And because he is consistent in sharing feedback with his mentee, his voice becomes the shoulders his mentee can stand on. His words compound the level of trust in their relationship. His observations open doors for his mentee to become more observant as well. To see life and himself in new ways.

Feedback shared in love produces self-confidence and growth. It leaves you feeling seen and encouraged.

Power of Asking Questions: Be the guide to help them figure life out

You've probably heard the saying, "Give a man a fish and you feed him for a day; teach a man to fish and you feed him for a lifetime." It is better to empower someone than to enable them. And nothing enables us more than those who are handing out easy answers and pre-packaged wisdom.

A goal of mentoring is to probe and prod and help your mentee find the answers using the tools and resources available to them. Circumventing their developmental process by presenting ideas and solutions to problems they are facing can create unhealthy dependencies and reluctance to develop their work ethic. Instead, spend more time listening to your mentee. Be quick to hear and slow to speak. Active listening can also help you figure out the "need behind the deed" of your mentee and help you guide them toward discovering the answer.

Mentoring is about helping your mentee grow in wisdom, character, and experience with a guide who loves them and is leading the way. Where are you sharing answers instead of asking your mentee questions?

Show How to Do Hard Things: Lead by example

Mentors aren't perfect—they're never meant to be. You are an example when you fail and try again, when you miss an appointment and apologize, when you're upset with your mentee and you take time to breathe before speaking, when you're tired but stay attentive. All of these things are okay. Many mentors feel like they have to be their absolute best around their mentee. But that doesn't help anyone. If anything, you are creating even more pressure and uneasiness for your mentee. They'll wonder, "Why is he so high-strung and put together? Is he always like this? Is this what I'm supposed to be like?"

The best mentors act like themselves in every setting they're in. The example they give is attainable, not "holier than thou." Their lives are attractive because of their flaws and need for grace. Their example is inviting because it appears to be a work in progress, not a work of perfection.

Take apologizing, for example. Everything is a teachable moment, even your own failures. How we fail determines how we get back up and grow. I can't think of a more important lesson for a mentee to learn from a mentor. Rather than focus on helping them process their own failures, find ways to demonstrate your own process through failure. If you didn't stay true to your word, acknowledge it and ask for forgiveness. If you messed up at work, or with your own kids, 'fess up to it and bring it into the light with your mentee. Let them see you fail and how you respond. Bring them in to your own process of responding to failure more than you expect them to show you theirs.

Apologizing to children is one of the greatest ways you can model humility but also honor the dignity of their personhood. Apologizing communicates value and respect, the building blocks of trust. By apologizing to children, we humble ourselves and raise them up.

Praying for Your Mentee: Ministry without prayer is the greatest form of arrogance

God wants mentors to hope more and enter into His joy for our mentee's lives. God is passionate about them! He has a calling and a plan for them no one else can fill. He has knit them together, hedged them in on the left and right, and He has made you their mentor. Do you feel a sense of responsibility? Do you see the depth of stewardship God is calling you to?

Prayer will bring you back into the reality of His sovereignty over your life and your mentee's life. Prayer will guide your heart toward God's heart for your mentee. What does God see in them that you can't see? What dreams does God have for their life, their future family, their children?

One way I remind myself to pray for my mentee is to write his name on my bathroom mirror with an expo marker. I also have his picture on my fridge so my family can pray for his family. Praying for your mentee helps you be a more consistent mentor.

What are your prayers for your mentee? What scriptures have influenced them the most? Where has God answered your prayers? What are you believing for your mentee in this season? Carve out regular time to pray for your mentee, trusting that God is more in control than we are.

When you pray, you can ask God to do the impossible, to change your mentee's story, and to break off generational cycles. Ask God for a vision of what He has for their future. Ask God what your role is in their life. Ask God for an encouragement to share.

Being a mentor is a privilege given to us by God. Without prayer, we will miss the weight and glory of what God is calling us to. God doesn't need you, but He chose you. Step forward into your role prayerfully, asking for His direction. The Holy Spirit is the master mentor. He will bring to mind scriptures, remind you of promises, and fill you with spiritual strength to remain faithful as a mentor.

Include Them: Don't take the simple things for granted

You may find it a struggle to relate to your mentee and to find common ground. My encouragement would be to consider inviting your mentee to do ordinary things together.

Ordinary things become cool when you do them with your mentor. Mentees are hungry for two things: food and relationship. It just so happens food and relationships are two primary ways humans have made memories together for all eternity.

Take the mundane errands you are already planning to do alone, and make them into memories for your mentee. One of the best things I ever did with one of my mentees was take him on my Sunday grocery store run each week. One day I asked him, "Why do you like to come to the grocery store with me?"

"I don't have anything else to do, Coach. I'm thirteen."

What may seem boring to you may end up being the highlight of their week.

Be Consistent: Under-promise, overdeliver

When you first start in a mentor relationship, you will feel tempted to expedite the process. You'll want to spend the first few meetings asking your mentee 100 questions. Instead, pace yourself and your questions. Don't force it or move too quickly when he or she doesn't respond immediately. It may not be because your question isn't being considered. Your mentee needs time to think. Let them take their time. Shoot for depth over breadth.

Relationships need time. You can't build trust in a month.

Under-promising and overdelivering is crucial in mentor relationships, particularly if you're mentoring a kid who has been let down by a significant relationship in the past, like his father.

One of the greatest things mentors can do is consistently show up. When it comes to deciding on the frequency and duration of your mentor interactions, only commit to what you have capacity for based on the foreseeable future. There is a cost to starting a mentor relationship. Be sure you've considered how it will affect your schedule, your family, your work, and your emotional capacity.

Are you fulfilling your commitment, but feel stressed out at your meetings? Do you find yourself checking your phone, answering emails, worrying about work or home while being with your mentee? Chances are you need to re-evaluate your commitment and make some changes. To over-deliver on your commitment, mentors need margin to keep their minds present and hearts engaged, actively listening to their mentee when they're together.

Enter Their World: Make what's important to them important to you

Mentors who enter into the world of their mentees will bear more fruit than those who expect their mentees to rise to theirs. This is a kingdom principle. God's light shines upon and blesses those who humble themselves and will kneel down to see life from their mentee's point of view. This is how compassion grows naturally. Jesus got down on this level for us.

Mentors always ask me for tips on how to keep the attention of their mentees. I tell them they're going about it the wrong way. The goal is not to get their attention. The goal is to give them yours. What does that mean? Figure out how to reassemble a Beyblade with precision. Brush up on your Mario Kart skills. Download Fortnite on your phone and learn the dance moves. Eat chicken nuggets again. Take the goofy up a notch and learn how to play as a kid again. This will help you start appreciating what your mentee values and begin seeing things from his or her perspective.

Communicate Often: Don't help them assume the worst

Clear communication is essential. When there is ambiguity in your communication with your mentee, it gives the devil an opportunity to lie to your mentee. Because of his past, fears will arise if you don't communicate in a clear, reassuring, and simple way. These lies will include fears like you will fail them, you say one thing but mean another, and won't do what you promise.

You must over-communicate with your mentee. Text when you're leaving and what time you'll arrive to pick them up. This will remove fear and doubt that you will cancel on them last minute. When you have a tough conversation, clearly state you are not mad and you are not going to leave. When you take your mentee to do activities outside the house, honor the family by communicating what you will be doing, where, and when you will be home.

Create Experiences: Make memories

Shoot for experiences over things. Kids don't need more things. They need more of our attention. If the only thing you have to show for your last mentor meeting is a heartfelt memory, you've succeeded. Memories may seem fleeting, but as you store them up in your mentee's mind, you are reminding him he's loved.

You are re-minding him. These positive, relational memories can rewire synapses in their brain that have become damaged by any number of traumatic experiences—words said or unsaid, or doubts they've held for years.

So go to the same restaurant every time you go out. That will be your place where you can order "the usual." Create holiday or birthday traditions. Your mentee will remember these when they are older. Teach how to make pancakes or banana bread or grill. Go sledding. Rake the leaves off the neighbor's yard together. Let your mentee teach you one of their hobbies. Go on a bike ride or hike. Be intentional in creating experiences that will make memories your mentee can hold on to for years to come.

Be Careful with Labels: Focus on where they're going not where they've been

A supporter of our nonprofit would introduce me using words that, while his heart was pure and intentions good, hurt me every time. He would say, "This is Zach. He runs a great nonprofit which helps fatherless kids. Zach was fatherless and overcame it, and now he's helping other fatherless kids as well."

While everything he said was true, his words reminded me of where I had been instead of focusing on where I am going. I don't necessarily think my friend was wrong in the way he introduced me, but

I think there's a better way. An introduction could instead be, "This is Zach. He runs a great nonprofit which supports kids who have some obstacles in their life. He's giving kids the same thing he received; love and support from a mentor, which transformed his life and put him on a path of success." Which one do you think is more honoring?

I've heard mentors introduce mentees and use words like poor, drugs, failure, and thug. No one wants to be called those even if it's true. How would it make you feel if someone talked about the worst parts of you when introducing you to strangers?

Don't call a kid poor. Instead of saying your mentee used drugs, say he's overcome some issues in his past. If he failed school, that's really no one's business but his own. Please never use the word thug. Use words that build up instead of tear down. There is a way of giving God glory without spotlighting the specific difficulties they have had in the past. Let them tell their story to whoever they choose if they want to. It's their story to tell anyways.

When talking about your mentee, always ask yourself if you are honoring them, their past, and their future with your words. Your words matter and can be the roadmap to a successful future for your mentee.

Creating Boundaries: Take care of yourself first

I have a friend named Kyle who mentors youth on the northeast side of Oklahoma City. He works with a lot of kids who have various needs and require continuous support. Kyle also has a wife and three kids at home. On any given day, Kyle is asked to help families in need in the community he serves. Early in his career, he would answer his phone at all hours to help his neighbors out.

One day, Kyle's wife came to him and said, "I know you love helping people and really care a lot about your job. But I feel like you love them more than you love me and the kids. You spend more time with them than you do us. I haven't had a date with you in months, but anytime someone calls you for help, you go running."

Kyle was convicted by the words of his sweet wife and promised to only answer the phone during work hours and to leave it turned off on the weekends.

The next day was a Sunday and Kyle and his family were sitting down for family lunch after church. That's when the phone rang. It was Kyle's mentee, James, calling to ask Kyle to come to his house to help him with something. Kyle was staring at his wife as the request came through the phone.

He simply said, "Look James, I love you, but I can't help you today. Try calling someone else, buddy. I will call you tomorrow morning to check in on you, but I need to be with my family today."

James was furious and hung up the phone without saying goodbye.

Kyle worried about James all night, but did his best to give his attention to his family. First thing the next morning, Kyle called James to ask if he was ok.

"James, is everything ok?"

"Uh, yeah. What are you talking about?"

"Well you called yesterday and said you needed help. Is everything cool?"

"Oh, that. Don't worry about it. I got it all figured out."

It is healthy to set boundaries with your mentee. Our mentoring organization has found the best way to set healthy boundaries is to clearly communicate them to your mentee and what he or she can expect from you. It is okay not to return every single text and to not answer every call as long as you tell them at the start, "If I don't answer your text, know I still care for you. Sometimes I am away from my phone. But I will reply as soon as I can."

Some of our mentees will unknowingly abuse the fact that you are there and care for them. They aren't doing this maliciously. Maybe they are just lonely and bored and you're the first person they think to call. Examples of this might include:

- Calling you just to chat late at night.
- Texting you multiple times during the work day until you answer.

Our advice to you is to set clear boundaries in the relationship with your mentee and stick to them. Examples of this might include:

- Saturday is the day I am with my family. I will not answer

texts or calls on Saturdays.
- I will not answer calls or texts past 8:00 at night.

You will need to say no to your mentee, in a gentle way, from time to time. You are not your mentee's only friend, chauffeur, or hangout buddy. You have other priorities and people who come before your mentee. If you are the best mentor in the world, but do so at the expense of spending time with your family, that is not a win. Keep appropriate boundaries which help you win in all areas of life.

Talking About Your Past:
Vulnerability creates vulnerability

There is power in a person's testimony. One of the best ways to teach a mentee the right path is to be open and honest about the mistakes and failures you have had in your own life. There is, however, wisdom in what to share and how much to share.

For example, if your mentee is navigating alcohol and drugs and you have experience in this topic, you can say, "I went through the same thing when I was your age and I know how it feels. Can I tell you what I learned from that experience?"

Please use wisdom and discernment in sharing your past. Do not glorify your sins or poor choices or make the focus about you. When in doubt, ask a seasoned mentor who can guide you through the process. This is another benefit of being associated with a mentoring organization.

Correcting Sinful Behavior: Rules for Correcting

When it comes to teens and pre-teens, the saying goes, "You must earn the right to be heard." When confronting destructive patterns in a child's life, here are some things I have learned:

Rule #1: Is Trust Established

Before you even consider having hard conversations with your mentee, you must ask yourself, "Do I have their trust?" A kid doesn't care what you know until he knows you care.

Having a hard conversation too early can actually set your relationship back a long ways if it goes poorly. How quickly trust is grown is dependent on your actions and their past. Typically, the younger they are, the fewer walls they have up. If the mentee is older, it might take a little longer to earn the right to be heard because they've been through a lot.

Rule #2: Pick Your Battles

As a mentor, you have to pick your battles. Is this a life or death issue? Will this lead your mentee to bigger sins that could have serious life consequences? Is this out-of-the-ordinary for the majority of teens? Bring these before the Lord and keep the big picture in mind! While all sins lead to death and prohibit life to the fullest, you also have to be wise and patient and bring up these sensitive issues as the Holy Spirit prompts you.

Rule #3: Prepare Wisely

Pray before you engage in a difficult conversation. Ask the Lord, "What do You want me to say?" and "Lord, please give me Your heart and compassion to help me communicate love to my kid."

Choose your timing. It's not the best idea to rebuke or bring up unwise decisions in the middle of having a great time with your mentee or when he or she is having a particularly tough day. Have the conversation toward the end of the hang-out as opposed to the beginning. One time I took a student on a walk and brought up a tough topic. It did not go well and we still had twenty minutes left on our walk back!

Gauge your own emotional levels. Make sure you are in an emotionally and spiritually stable spot before you engage in this battle. While no time feels like a good time to have a tough conversation, we can be strategic to set ourselves and our child up for success.

Lastly, the environment matters. Make sure it is in a quiet place where you can have a serious conversation.

. . .

Rule #4: Ask Permission

Instead of blurting out what they are doing wrong, say something like: "You know I love you and want the best for you, right? Well, I've noticed some things that might keep you from being the best version of you. Do you mind if I share those with you?"

If the mentee says yes, proceed. If their answer is no, let it go and trust God will provide another opportunity for you or someone else to address the issue.

If your mentee is doing something dangerous and could impact his or her future in a negative way, pray about stepping in. You can keep your mentee safe while understanding the relationship and foundation of trust must be protected. In most cases, it is vital we consider the relationship and good standing with your mentee higher than the need to correct them. This is another reason to be connected with a mentoring organization as they can be your sounding board for how to proceed.

Rule #5: Be Gentle

Asking questions and getting them to think about the *why* behind their actions typically works better than talking *at* them. No one likes being lectured. Stories work better than advice as it helps them see the big picture.

Be mindful of your tone. If the child hears you as judgmental, harsh, or angry, they will probably shut down or get angry. We want children to know we are for them and believe the best about them.

Above all else, trust that the Lord loves your mentee even more than you do and is ultimately responsible for transforming the child's heart. Your goal is to show love. We care more about the heart than the actions. Just like how the Lord handles us, we strive to give an abundance of grace to the kids we mentor.

Providing for Them: They need love above all

It is okay if your mentee doesn't have all the amenities you are used to. This sounds weird, but it is okay if your mentee sleeps on the couch and receives only one gift at Christmas. Your normal might not be their normal.

This is one reason why it is wise to mentor under an organization or church as they can provide for necessities if needed—like a bed to sleep in, and guidance or assistance for opportunities like signing a child up for little league or summer camp. But know it is okay if he doesn't have those things. That is not your responsibility. Love, attention, and guidance are more important than a bed or a summer camp experience.

Focus on Them:
The development process of the teen brain

When we talk about earning our mentees attention, we have to understand where their brains are in this development process. The Prefrontal Cortex is the thinking part of the brain. It's large. This part of the brain is used for decision-making, relationships, learning, reading, remembering, focusing, solving problems, and is where our personality is developing. This part of the brain is the most immature in children, and takes years to develop. 25 years in fact. In adolescence this part of the brain goes through a kind of reset. This is where synaptic pruning is introduced, where meaningful brain connections are strengthened by pruning weaker connections in the brain. When your teenager pitches a fit and acts like a three year old, the prefrontal cortex is to blame.

Brain development in this season is heavily influenced by a child's surroundings, attachments, and more. Kids from hard places live at the intersection of a number of injustices which affect their development. What hindrances have kept their brain from growing? What obstacles will that present for them later on in life? Allow the Lord to stir compassion in your heart for the child you are mentoring. If you are always feeling frustrated about how the kid you're investing in is acting, or treating you in the relationship, remind yourself their brain is still developing.

Earn Their Attention by Giving Them Yours

When you think of Jesus descending, becoming flesh and bone, do you see it as God seeking our attention, or Him giving us His? The God of the Bible sought us out. He listens. More than anything, Jesus reveals how much God cares for us. God offers us His attention so we have the choice to offer Him our own. If we know someone is interested in us, it's a lot easier to open up.

When we give our mentee attention, we're able to ask better questions. It's hard to ask someone good questions if you aren't looking to learn more about them, their responses to life situations, their hobbies, and more. You can learn so much about a person just by watching them.

Earn Their Attention by Finding Out What Brings Them Joy

What do they like and how can you connect with them in it? When we find common ground and feel connected to another person, we're more open to their influence. This makes it easy for them to listen and interact with you.

So, get curious. What is going on in the brain of the child you're mentoring? What questions do they have? What makes them wonder? Teachers know this already. When kids are curious, they're much more likely to stay engaged.

Ask good questions to not only find out more about your mentee, but to also help them figure out as much as possible about themselves. What are they good at? Where do they have talent and passion? What types of environment or activities does your mentee thrive in? What makes them come alive? Together, you and your mentee can figure out these answers.

Earn Their Attention by Commanding it, Not Demanding It

Jesus never demanded attention, His life commanded it. There's a difference between someone walking in the room and saying, "Hey! Learn from me! I'm awesome!" and another who lives in such a way it draws the attention of others and creates curiosity.

We live in an age of distraction. Just because you say, "Hey, listen to me," doesn't mean a child or teen will. They may never have had training in how to listen well. Take time to teach them how to listen. Find a resource to walk them through. Just because a kid is ten years old doesn't mean they are ten years old developmentally speaking.

Listening is a life discipline we should be constantly growing in. For some of our kids, that part of their brain is underdeveloped. When we speak with adults, we expect them to be respectful and listen when we speak and give us cues that they're listening. This doesn't mean we always listen perfectly, but we try to listen because it's respectful and shows people you value them. But if children grow up in homes where they are not listened to when they speak up, or ignored when they ask a question, they may need to practice how listening and interacting works.

Another way to get their attention is to reflect their feelings. This may sound something like, "You are angry," or "You don't want to eat dinner," or "You hate bedtime and you wish you could stay up later," or "You're upset because the kids at school called you names," and "Man, that is so frustrating when you try so hard and it doesn't turn out the way you want." Tapping into their emotions builds the connection with your mentee. There is nothing more comforting to a child than a mentor who listens and understands.

Practical Listening:

Ask good questions:

- You may be the first non-family member who has taken the time to push through all the distractions, ask them good questions, and fight for their attention. And by the way, good questions aren't easy to answer. So if you're asking good questions, their inability to respond quickly isn't because their wheels aren't turning, it might be because they've never even turned. Good questions cultivate our minds. An article on Fast Company's website stated that if our brain is thinking about an answer to a question, it can't think about anything else. So when we ask our mentees good questions, we are helping their brains to grow in focus.

- Behavioral scientists have found simply asking questions about future decisions significantly influences those decisions. So when we ask good questions to kids from hard situations, we're planting seeds.
- Believe the best about your mentee. Give them the benefit of the doubt.

Help kids listen:

- Connect with eye contact before you speak.
- One question at a time. Use few and simple words.
- Don't "should" on them. This means avoid telling them what they should do. Instead, give context and an explanation as to why that action is not good for them.
- Be more assertive and less optional. Giving direction for what you want them to do is not a bad thing. It's actually safe.
- Make every effort to stop what you are doing to listen to them

CHAPTER ELEVEN

Seasons of Mentoring

THE GOAL IS for mentors to be in the life of their mentee for a long, long time. However, that doesn't always happen.

Here's a few things to keep in mind:

- Every relationship and every timeline is different regarding the seasons of mentoring. Some relationships might go through all of the seasons listed below and some may not. Some seasons might last a long time, while others are short.
- Resist the temptation to compare your mentoring relationship with your peers. Every kid is different. Every mentor is different. Every relationship is unique.
- Age and maturity matters. You aren't going to have deep conversations with a third grader no matter how good your mentoring relationship is going. Also, not all teenagers and young adults are equal. It takes a certain type of maturity to have a quality relationship, and not all mentees have that maturity.
- Time is the most important thing in any relationship. That being said, when your mentee is younger, the quantity of time you spend with your mentee is more important than the quality of time. Every kid it is different, but for most, quantity

over quality time lasts from about six to fourteen years old. Once they enter their teenage years, it flips. Then it becomes more quality time over quantity of time. You might not see them as often, but the quality of your conversations are more in depth and important.

The Honeymoon Stage
First Six Months to a Year

New is fun! All is good! Typically the mentee loves his mentor and puts on his best act to impress. He wants to show you how cool he is and make sure he puts on a good enough show to keep you around.

Expectations are sky high. Mentors might expect their mentee to share her entire life story, fears, dreams, and everything during the first meeting.

The mentor pulls out all the stops for his mentee. He takes the mentee to the coolest places and visits him more often than he thought he would. This mentoring thing is easy!

The heart is good. The intentions are good. But can this pace be kept up?

Early on as a mentoring organization, we didn't have too many rules and regulations. To say we were flying by the seat of our pants would have been an insult to my pants. We simply found a kid who wanted a mentor and found him a mentor. That's how we matched up Travis and Tyree.

Travis was an all-in mentor. His life had been changed by a mentor and he wanted to pay it forward with a kid in our community. Travis pulled out all the stops early on in his relationship with Tyree and was definitely the coolest mentor we had. But, with a young family and a demanding job, I wondered how long he could keep this up.

He would pick Tyree up every week and take him to some unique experience or some super fun outing. At the end of every trip Travis would stop at Wal-Mart and give Tyree five dollars so Tyree could go pick out a toy or some candy. It was a great way to bond with Tyree. Until it wasn't.

One day, Travis was hanging out with Tyree when his wife called. She told him they had dinner plans they forgot about. "No problem," said Travis. "I'll just drop Tyree off and come on home. We should be able to make dinner."

When Tyree heard this, he asked about their weekly trip to Wal-Mart. Travis explained the situation, but the only thing Tyree could focus on was his candy and toy. Tyree totally lost his cool and started screaming curse words at Travis. This created an obstacle they both had to overcome.

A new mentoring relationship is exciting. There is a tendency for a mentor to come into the relationship like Santa Claus, giving all this cool stuff and making fun memories. Subconsciously, it is easy to believe you have exactly what this kid needs to succeed. You want to meet their every need and give them every opportunity to succeed in life. Your heart is good, even if your actions might be made out of ignorance.

Main lie: I am the answer to all my mentee's issues. It will always go great because I am such a good mentor.

The enemy loves to toss this lie to you. He also lies to both you and your mentee that you must behave in a certain way in order to be accepted. It causes both to abandon your true self and be someone you're not—a hard game to play for the long run. When beginning, we must observe our actions and ask, "Is this really who I am? If not, am I trying to be someone other than who I am to impress my mentee?"

You are enough. The Lord didn't mess up when He made you and He has paired you with your mentee for a specific reason.

The Wall Stage
Six to Thirty-six Months (depending on mentee's past and age, but typically during adolescence)

For some kids who have never experienced a loving relationship, they can feel freaked out when things start to get comfortable. Internally, they might think, "I've started to trust this person. I've never done that before. And it scares me." Or "The last time I trusted an adult they hurt me." Or, they will say, "I've been burned so many times, I'm going to make this relationship as hard as I possibly can to see if this mentor will stick around." So, they begin to build a wall to protect their heart.

This is when mentors begin to wonder things like, "Why isn't he talking to me? Why won't she open up to me? When did he move and why doesn't his cell phone number work? She told me she'd show up and she's nowhere to be found. This is really hard and he doesn't even seem to like me."

This is where it gets real. The honeymoon is over and you both are finding out who each other really is. This is also where you start to understand your mentee's story.

This is where we begin to see the world our kids live in. Perhaps your kid moves schools or his cell phone number changes. Maybe you find out your child deals with food scarcity and general instability at home. You learn about the stories and experiences which made them who they are today. You hear their past and understand the traumas they have potentially gone through. This is where you figure out the kid you mentor has some major issues or hurts in their life. You see him when he shuts down or have sat through a conversation when he doesn't open up to you.

Main lies: I don't have what it takes to succeed. He doesn't even like hanging around me.

I've experienced the wall stage with a number of kids. For some, it lasts weeks and for some it has lasted years. Looking back, what the Lord was doing during that season was not only changing the heart of my mentee to trust me, but He was changing my heart as well. He was teaching me how to persevere and to keep tossing seeds even though I wasn't seeing fruit.

Stephen has been a fantastic mentor. But the first few years with his mentee, Marcus, were tough. Marcus didn't give Stephen much attention for the first couple years. And this was really hard on Stephen. It seemed like every time I spoke to Stephen, he was down on his relationship with Marcus. It got so bad at times, Stephen almost quit.

Then the weirdest thing happened. I contacted Marcus after my conversation with Stephen to see where he was in the relationship. Marcus said he absolutely loved Stephen and went on and on about how much fun he was having when they would spend time together. Marcus opened up to me and even thanked me for pairing him with Stephen.

Stephen thought his relationship with Marcus was a failure because of how Marcus was reacting to him. But here's the thing: you can't trust your mentee's reaction. You never know what the Lord is doing in a kid's heart. During this time, the main thing a mentor needs to do is trust that the Lord is up to something in the kid's heart.

When a mentor encounters a wall when building a trusting relationship, the best thing to do is continue to show up in the life of the kid. The height of the wall is a direct reflection upon the mentee's past and what they have experienced. The higher the wall; the deeper the hurt.

It is not a mentor's job to break down the wall. The mentee built the wall and they will tear the wall down when they are good and ready. Relationships move at the speed of trust, and the mentee will give you his trust in his own timing. I believe every time you show up, every time you speak a word of encouragement or tell your mentee you are glad to be with him or her, one brick is coming off the wall. We just need to persevere.

While the wall stage is happening, we encounter a major decision. And that is our next stage...

The Fight or Flight Stage
Thirty-one Minutes or Six to Twelve Months after the Wall Stage

When you are in relationship with someone long enough, some things start to come to the surface. Issues about their past might slip out in a casual conversation. Dreams and fears might pop up in the middle of a meal together. The longer you hang out with someone, the more you find out about them. Everyone puts on their best behavior on the first few dates. You are quick to share all the good about you. But the bad? The bad usually only comes out after it's been a while. You can't hide those in the dark forever.

In the fight or flight stage, you know who your mentee is and he or she knows who you are. There are no more secrets. This is the time when you as the mentor decide if you are really up for this. Perhaps you are frustrated that mentoring isn't what you thought it would be. Maybe, instead of showing improvement, your mentee is actually getting worse. When this happens, the mentor has a choice.

- Fight: Do I continue and trust that God will move through our relationship?
- Flight: Do I quit because I think this relationship is hopeless?

If you decide to fight for the relationship and stick it out, thick or thin, you will realize you have to fight against the lies of the enemy. This is a war. You will see how you have to make some sacrifices because your mentee is more hurt than you thought. You have to know the life of a mentee might not turn out how you wanted, and that's ok. You will understand that the relationship isn't as easy as you thought it would be.

Main lie: This is a waste of time. It's not working and it will never work.

In your mentoring relationship, there will be times when you fall down. There will be misunderstandings, frustrations, and disappointments. But don't let mishaps and bumps in the road overthrow you. Proverbs 24:16 says, "for the righteous falls seven time and rises again, but the wicked stumble in times of calamity."

Mentors must contend for the relationship. This means you make a conscious decision to face the adversity which comes from your mentee's past and hurt. Your mentee didn't build a wall for no reason. Continuing to show up and fight through the hurt and lies will show your mentee she can trust you and you want what is best for her.

If you choose to endure and continue to invest into your mentee, soon you will reap the benefits of your actions. If we are able to fight through conflicts and arguments, there is a good chance those experiences will actually bring you closer to your mentee.

This leads to the next season.

The Genuine Relationship Stage
Fourteen Years of Age to Mid-Twenties

This is what you actually signed up for, it just may have taken a little longer to get to than you thought. This is when your mentee begins to believe you are the real deal. Your mentee trusts you and opens up. The Lord has cultivated a heart for your mentee and spending time with them brings you a ton of joy. Your mentee starts to truly understand that you back up your talk with action. You are trustworthy. You do what you say you'll do. Your mentee is starting to mature, and that is a really big deal.

Your mentee believes you will show up even when he doesn't act perfect and love him no matter what. He knows you have his back no matter what. Your mentee might even start to feel free to ask questions and disagree with you. Your mentee truly begins to feel accepted and loved for who she is. The wall is coming down and the heart is beginning to open. Your mentee begins to let you into his life and might even show his appreciation from time to time.

Your heart begins to change, too. You truly care for your mentee and enjoy spending time with him. You focus more on quality time instead of on deeds or progress and understand that only the Lord can change someone's heart.

This is the season to gently challenge them and hold them accountable as the Spirit leads. You can "call them up" by having harder conversations about serious issues. You celebrate the small wins as he grows in positivity and perseverance. You might even begin to see some fruit. You might let him or her into your life a little more as you find it appropriate.

I will always remember when my mentee said, "I love you, too" when I dropped him off at his apartment. Or the time when he texted me out of nowhere to see how I was doing. For a teenager to think of someone other than himself and to initiate communication with an adult is something I consider a major win.

Of course, there are still potential issues in this season. One of the main issues is fighting for the time of the mentee. As he grows older, other things begin to take priority in his life. Romantic relationships, sports, friends, work, and school play major roles in the life of your mentee.

Main lies: This kid doesn't need me. He's not calling me as much as he used to and things are different. Our relationship isn't a priority for him.

But because you are in a place of health, you and your mentee can effectively deal with conflict in a productive way. If it does derail the relationship, it's not for long. This is where we must continue to be patient, pursue no matter what, and be thankful for the time we get with them, no matter how limited.

This is what we like to call a mutual relationship. He or she has buy-in and puts forth effort—just like you. Both mentor and mentee bring something to the table.

Things get real, and this looks like it's heading toward…

The Life-Long Relationship Stage

Our desire is for this to be a life-long relationship. This is the dream for all mentor/mentee pairings. We hope your kids call your mentee "brother" or "sister." We hope your wife loves your mentee as her own child. We hope you will be the best man at your mentee's wedding. We hope you will be there when he or she has kids of their own. Maybe your mentee will name his child after you. We want your mentee to be a pallbearer at your funeral. This life-long relationship might not happen, and that's okay. But the potential is there. Relationships change lives. That's how generational curses turn into generational blessings.

In this stage, you are still responsible for the pursuit of the relationship as most young adults haven't mastered the art of initiation or asking for feedback yet. If they don't pursuit you, it's not because they don't care for you, but instead it is because they aren't mature enough yet. Don't stop. If you are confused if they want to hang out with you, just ask them. Weeks and months can go by without contact with your mentee, but that's okay. There is grace. You know they love you and you know you love them. Continue to show up, pray for them, and wait for the Lord to transform their life in His perfect timing. You never know what the Lord will do or when He'll do it.

***

No two mentoring relationships are the same. Each one ebbs and flows and has highs and lows. Kids mature. Mentors grow more patient. You never know what the Lord is going to do in you, your mentee, and your relationship.

If you are in a mentoring relationship for a prolonged period of time, the Lord will change your heart. He will show you new ways to love like He loves. While we never know the specific circumstances each relationship will encounter, having an idea of the different mentoring seasons can help you navigate and prepare. When you experience something together, good or bad, it has a way of growing you closer. It unifies and gives you a new appreciation for that person.

CHAPTER TWELVE
Success as a Mentor

TERRANCE IS A great kid in our mentoring program, but he has an anger problem. From time to time, his temper got the best of him and he would get into a fight with another kid. I decided to spend some time with Terrence to encourage him and give him some wisdom. The meeting went great. I felt like Terrence really heard what I had to say. I believed true change took place. Terrence and I left on good terms and I was proud I was able to make an impact on his decision-making in this area.

Life was good.

The next day, I found out Terrance got in another fight.

What? Didn't we just talk about this? I thought he learned his lesson!

Discouragement. Disappointment. Feeling like you aren't making a difference. Keep in mind the enemy will do whatever he can to keep you from showing unconditional love to one of God's children. He wants to make you think you aren't making an impact and that this kid is a lost cause.

How you view, think about, and evaluate your relationship with the student you are mentoring will determine what kind of relationship you have. Simply put, if you think your mentoring relationship is successful, you are more likely to keep at it. If you feel like it is a failure, you are more likely to quit.

Mentors spend so much time, energy, and emotional capacity on their relationship with their mentee. They want to know, "Have I made an impact? Is this working?" But the answer is more complicated than we think.

People are People, Not Projects

We all want to feel successful when we put our time and energy into something. It feels really good to solve a hard problem or accomplish a goal at work. Most of the time, success happens because of the following equation:

Hard work + perseverance = Success

That's how the world works. Often, it's how our jobs work. It doesn't matter if you are a teacher, a salesman, or a scientist, you will be praised and seen as successful if you follow the equation above.

I often see people try to fit mentoring into the same formula. Unfortunately, what works in society does not work in mentoring. An easy trap to fall into is unconsciously seeing the kid you mentor as a project instead of a person. The equation is expected to go something like this:

Spend time with a kid + teaching him wise ways = Life Transformation

Mentoring simply doesn't work that way. I have mentored two students this past decade. One is in college making A's and B's and one just got released from prison. I did nothing different. I did the exact same thing with both students. Two totally different outcomes. Every person is different. Each person comes from a different background with a different personality and different priorities.

Remember your mentee is not a project, he is a person—a person with a story and a background and a future. There is no such thing as a formula to success when it comes to mentoring.

The question isn't, "Am I having success as a mentor?" The question we should be asking ourselves is, "Is this kid's life better because of our mentoring relationship?" If the answer is yes, even in the slightest bit, we are on the right track.

Instead of focusing on our success, let's focus on the kid. It's not about us.

Here are some things to remember to protect your mind from becoming discouraged in mentoring:

It is a Marathon

In Psalm 103:7, God says He made known His ways to Moses. In Hebrew, the phrase "His ways" literally means "to walk" or "to journey." I picture Moses and God taking a walk together, just making the journey one step at a time. That is a perfect picture of mentoring—a long, slow walk in the same direction—taking a journey with someone and teaching them all they need to know along the way. Mentoring, just like a relationship with God, is a marathon—not a sprint.

Suzanne Wallace is a hero of mine. She is a seventy year old white woman who loves Jesus with all of her heart. She has dedicated herself to mentoring kids from hard places in East Dallas. When I asked her what one piece of advice she would give to new mentors, she said, "It takes time."

A few years back, Suzanne was mentoring a teenaged girl named CeCe who wasn't making the best decisions. Suzanne decided it was time for a heart-to-heart conversation with CeCe, so she asked her to come over and have a chat. When CeCe arrived, Suzanne drew three circles on paper, one inside of the other. The smallest circle, she labeled You and God. The next circle out was labeled Your Closest Friends and Positive Influences. The largest circle was labeled Marginal Friends and Bad Influences.

Suzanne said, "The goal is that this first circle of friends points you to God. They help influence you to grow with the Lord and to honor Him with your actions. Then you guys, as a group, can go and positively influence your other friends. But your problem is you've got these circles reversed. You surround yourself with friends who are bad influences, so much to the point where those negative relationships are pushing out your positive relationships. Do you understand?"

When Suzanne looked up, CeCe was rolling her eyes and fuming with anger. She tapped her foot, her arms crossed, and looked like she wanted to be anywhere else on earth but at that kitchen table with Suzanne. It seemed like CeCe didn't hear a word Suzanne said.

Fast forward six years and CeCe has radically given her life to Jesus. She even decided to go to a discipleship training school after high school. After the training school, she got a job at a local church working with their high school students.

One day, Suzanne gets a call from CeCe who wanted some advice on how to deal with Julie, an eighteen year old who is making some pretty bad decisions. CeCe was worried about Julie, so she took her out to dinner to talk about her life. After the meeting, CeCe called Suzanne and said "I took her out to dinner and it didn't make a bit of difference. I even drew those circles you once drew for me and it didn't work!"

Even though it hadn't looked like it, Cece had listened to Suzanne. It just took a little longer than expected to sink in.

We're in it for the long haul. Failure today doesn't mean failure tomorrow. Just because we don't see fruit doesn't mean the seeds aren't growing. Sometimes what you say today won't actually register until years down the road.

Some miles are a lot tougher than others. You'll have seasons where it's uphill. Seasons where it's downhill. Pace yourself on the downhills. Push through on the uphills.

Celebrate Every Improvement

One day, the Lord challenged me to be more gentle with our students. This is one of my biggest areas to grow in. In the program, I witnessed a student go into his normal rhythm of getting mad, making fun of a kid, and then shouting at him. I pulled him to the side to talk to him. But before I started the discussion, he said, "Coach, I didn't hit him!"

Right there I had a choice. I could have said "You're right, but you got mad, made fun of him, and shouted at him." Or I could have said, "You're right. That's an improvement and I'm really proud you are taking steps in the right direction! Now, let's talk about how else you can become the man I know you can be."

We must ask ourselves, "What's the trajectory?" If a kid makes a 50 on a test, is that a good thing? Well, what did he make last week? If he made a 30 last week and a 50 this week, he's on the right trajectory. Maybe next week he can aim for a 70!

A goal should be to always be moving up, even if barely moving. If you move an inch every week for a decade, you might look up and be rather impressed with the amount of ground you've covered.

It is hard to improve. It is so much harder to improve when your accomplishments don't get celebrated. If your mentee achieves a goal or improves in a certain area, point it out and celebrate. Celebration and encouragement is fuel that will keep your mentee going. Speak phrases like, "I am so proud of you," and "I knew you had what it took to do this," and "It makes me so happy to see you doing so well." These go a really long way in a mentoring relationship.

Our students need a lot of courage to go against the grain and fulfill their potential. Family issues, prior trauma, cultural pressures, and peer pressure can make it really hard for our mentees to improve. But they have you to cheer them on. You can pick them up when they fall down and speak words of identity and destiny over them to keep them going.

Celebrate the wins. Be your mentee's biggest fan.

Another Suzanne story is when Juan, a kid who she mentored thirty years ago shared his testimony at an organization's fundraiser. It was the first time she had seen Juan in a long, long time. Suzanne listened to Juan share his story about how he came to fall in love with Jesus Christ. Juan is now a banker in North Dallas and pursuing his Masters of Business.

Suzanne stared at this successful man and started to remember where Juan was when she first started mentoring him. Not only was Juan dealing drugs, but he was in upper-level management of this gang. His life was a mess and he was up to no good.

Suzanne then looked across the room and she saw Joe. She remembered how Joe was on his way to prison when he entered the program, but who now loves Jesus and is an artist working for the Dallas Mavericks. She sees Adrian, who was a drug dealer and worked under Juan back in the day. Today, he is a follower of Jesus and a small business owner. She sees Sergio, a real estate broker, who used to be another drug dealer in the community.

Never in a million years did Suzanne think those young boys who were up to no good would turn into who they are today, but the Lord had different plans.

Hard Can be Good

"Blessed is the man who remains steadfast under trial, for when he has stood the test he will receive the crown of life, which God has promised to those who love him (James 1:12, ESV)."

Contrary to popular belief, life isn't about avoiding obstacles. The key to life is not about making things easy. Tension is good. Suffering helps us grow in endurance and maturity. It helps us be steadfast and strong during the hard times. Our job as mentors is not to remove the obstacles, but to help our mentees learn how to overcome obstacles. It does our mentee no good if we remove the hurdles from the track. Instead, train them how to jump over the hurdles to get to the goal no matter what.

The hard things you go through with your mentee are opportunities to grow in character, endurance, and deepen your relationship with each other. Conflict and trials have a weird way of uniting people. Hard is good. Like a weightlifter who is trying to grow stronger muscles, sometimes you need to tear something up to rebuild it stronger. Difficult situations with your mentee can do just that. You are also teaching and giving your mentee tools to overcome difficulties. You are instilling confidence in their ability to be successful in life no matter what comes their way.

God loves when we face tension head on. It is a good thing when a trial comes and we don't let it discourage or deter us, but instead allow it to grow us. Facing difficulty is not a clear-cut sign the mentor relationship is failing. It may actually be a sign it's working. Difficulty is not failure. Difficulty is real relationship.

No matter how beneficial conflict and sufferings are, they are not fun in the moment. "For the moment all discipline seems painful rather than pleasant, but later it yields the peaceful fruit of righteousness to those who have been trained by it" (Hebrews 12:11, ESV).

One important thing to note when difficult situations arise: Be sure to affirm the relationship once the trial is over. Schedule the next hang out right then. Tell them you aren't going anywhere. Use your words to let them know you still love them.

If You Don't Quit, You Win

John began mentoring Drew and Luke early in elementary school. He watched them grow up into the wonderful men they are today. He went to their sporting events, took them out to eat weekly, and even took them on vacation to New York City. All in all, he was their mentor for over a decade and truly loved them with all his heart.

It was very odd when John quit mentoring Drew and Luke when they were sixteen and eighteen years old. Upon hearing John wasn't spending time with Drew and Luke anymore, I asked him what happened. He said, "They just didn't have time for me anymore. I guess they're too cool for me. They stopped answering my texts and phone calls, so I figured we're done."

I tracked down Drew and Luke and asked them about it. Their answer was, "I don't know why he stopped coming around. But whatever. I don't need him anymore anyways."

Years later, Drew and Luke still talk about how John gave up on them. It truly hurt them to the core and reminded them of the lie that they aren't worthy of love and attention. It reinforced the lie that men don't stick around.

If you are unclear about something regarding your mentee, be the bigger, more mature person and ask them about it. Be as bold as to say, "Hey, I feel like you don't like hanging out with me anymore. Is that true or am I off?" Don't assume. Bring those feelings and thoughts into the light so together you two can figure out what is truly going on.

Don't quit on your mentee. Obviously things like moving, having children of your own, and major life changes sometimes make it necessary to gently and respectfully find a new mentor for your mentee. But, if you can help it, don't quit for petty, immature reasons. Being a part of a supportive mentoring organization can equip and encourage you to persevere during the hard times, to stay positive, and not make assumptions. You must resist the lies the enemy will tell you.

***

One thing I believe with all my heart is God will use your mentoring relationship to better your mentee's life. It might not look the way you think it should, but I believe your investment will impact your mentee's heart in a positive way.

Mentoring can be a great way to actually put into practice the things we read in the Bible. Things like:

- It is not good for man to be alone, and mentoring creates relationship.
- Mentoring is a great way to love our neighbor and spread the Gospel through disciple-making.
- God sets the lonely in family, and you have the opportunity to do that as well with your mentee.
- For some of our mentees growing up without a father around, mentoring can serve the modern-day orphan and widow.
- We get to be like Jesus and never cast out our mentee.
- We get to lead our mentees out of the darkness and into the light. We get to be a light in the darkness and an example for others to follow.
- We get to lose our life and serve for the sake of our mentee and his future generations.
- We get to love one another.
- You get to be 2 Timothy 2:2: "And what you have heard from me in the presence of many witnesses entrust to faithful men, who will be able to teach others also" (ESV).

One of my favorite aspects of mentoring is you never know what the Lord is going to do with your mentee and your relationship with them. You never know what the future holds for your mentee. Maybe they will go to college and become wildly successful in business. Perhaps they will become a preacher and share the gospel with thousands. Maybe they will have a wife and a few kids who grow up in a stable, safe, and secure home where they are loved no matter what. Maybe his faithfulness to create a Godly home for his children produces kids who love the Lord and believe in themselves? Isn't that a huge win? I believe the people who will benefit the most from your mentoring relationship are actually the spouse and children of your mentee.

Your mentees' hard work of overcoming traumas, forgiving those who hurt them, and humbly submitting to a mentor will set their children and their children's children up for success in the future.

Your mentee is a world-changer and a history maker. They are shouting to their future generations, "You will never know what it is like to be alone. You will learn to love the things of the Lord and will fulfill your God-given potential!"

My favorite part of the parable of the sower is the last part: "As for what was sown on good soil, this is the one who hears the word and understands it. He indeed bears fruit and yields, in one case a hundredfold, in another sixty, and in another thirty (Matthew 13:23, ESV).

Your mentee will produce a crop. I know this because He who calls you is faithful. And God is for them, not against them. And His crop will be thirty, sixty, or a hundred times what you thought it would be. Your mentee will impact the world in ways you can't even imagine.

Generational sin will turn into generational blessing. The lonely will find family. Lives will be transformed. Ashes will turn into beauty and what is dead will become alive again. And God will do this all through the context of relationship.

There are millions of kids looking for someone to love them with the love of Jesus Christ, someone who will love them no matter what and just the way they are. And I believe you can do that. I believe you can show up when most wouldn't and I believe you have what it takes to be used by the Lord to transform a life. Just give Him your "yes" and trust He will do the rest of the work.

You can mentor.

Acknowledgements

First and foremost, I want to thank my beautiful wife, Sara, for walking with me through our mentoring journey. There is no one I'd rather do ministry with and there is no way I'd be the man I am today, doing what I'm doing, without you. Thank you for allowing me the time and space to write this book. I love you.

To both my mom and my dad: I hope I have walked the tightrope of honestly telling my story from my perspective while honoring you both with my words and actions. I love you both.

To my children, ZJ, Stephen, and Joanna, my world changers and history makers. I love you with all of my heart. It is my joy and passion to be the best father possible to you three.

To The Following Mentors:

All my Apollo coaches: Thanks for loving a jacked-up junior high kid. Your attention kept me from going off the deep end.

Bob Strader: Thank you for giving a kid who deserved no chance at leading a chance to lead. Thank you for pursuing me in my junk. Thank you for being there for me when I needed someone to be there for me.

Joel Busby: Thanks to the first guy in my life who was a Christian but also someone who I wanted to be like. By the way, what's your weakness?

Paul Gittemeier: Thank you for letting me sit at your table and watch you lead your family. Thank you for saying no to being my mentor and thank you for introducing me to Alex Louis.

Alex Louis: Thank you for asking me the hard questions. Thank you for calling me out. Thank you for making me better.

Don Finto: Thank you for kissing me on the cheek and for loving me no matter what.

Steve Allen: Man of God. Thank you for everything.

Scott Frost: Your leadership, humility, wisdom, intellect, and covering has played a massive part in my development as a man. Thank you.

Bryant Gullette: You stuck by me when few would. For that, I am forever thankful.

John Williams: Thank you for letting me into your life. Your transparency and vulnerability taught me more than you know. Thank you for cheering me on and for being in my corner. I have never regretted one morning I've spent with you.

To the following friends:

Brandon Horne: Doesn't matter what I have going on, I know I can count on you. You love me unconditionally. If that's not a best friend, I don't know what is.

Alex Eagle: Alexander. Older Brother. I remember sitting in your apartment in Fort Worth listening to John Mayer. "Hey Al. I think I love Jesus." You got me to Nashville and Jerusalem. You've been there every step of the way.

John Bower: Thank you for asking me to come to The Village Apartments for a Tuesday night men's Bible study. You are the best pastor I know.

John Kaserman: You taught me how to love the Lord. For that, I am forever grateful.

Justus Murimi: Young Steeze. My man. My running mate. My joy coach. Let's keep sharpening up each other.

Jason Purser: Thanks for always being up to talk about Jesus, El Jim, the Cowboys, mentoring, and the deeper things of life. When I need to have fun, I call you. Your music is still terrible, though.

Mac Macfarlan: Thanks for teaching me not to get offended. And thanks for letting me teach you how to dove hunt. Your belief in me means the world.

Joshua Flynt: Thanks for always having my back and for taking me to Dunkin' Donuts in 2009.

J Bry, Al, The Blurrr, and Adam: I am in ministry. The Lord is funny like that.

Thanks to Chad Lancaster, Clint Justice, Ricky Zorn, Greg Johnson, Jason Matthews, Rick Howard, and Jeremy Sain: I will forever be grateful for your leadership of me and Forerunner. You each had a part to play in this book and my life.

To Peter Louis and Ryan Casey Waller: Thanks for encouraging me to write and for being an example to follow.

To Caroline Tidwell, Beth Winter, Lauri Nagy, Stephen Murray, and

Darius Person: You make Forerunner what it is. I am beyond proud of you all and I fully trust you with this organization. Always be growing. Relationships change lives. More of Him, less of us.

Thank you, Estee Zandee and Leilani Squires, for your work editing this book. When in doubt, take it out! I need to send your parents a thank you card for creating such literary geniuses.

Thank you to the You Can Mentor community. Thank you for sharing your insight, experiences, and failures to help me become a better mentor. Here's to starting a mentoring movement!

Lastly, thank You Jesus for transforming my life. Never in a million years would I believe You could take a kid like me and use him for good. I love You more than anything. More of You, less of me.

About the Author

When Zach Garza was a kid heading down a dark path with no one to guide him, the Lord changed his life through mentoring. In 2010, after a career in teaching and coaching kids in low-income communities, Zach founded the *Forerunner Mentoring Program* in Dallas, Texas and now serves as the Vice President of expansion for *The Mentoring Alliance*. The Forerunner Mentoring Program daily invests in the lives of young people through mentoring relationships, after-school programming, and supporting single mothers. As the founder of the *You Can Mentor Network*, Zach equips and encourages mentors to build relationships with kids who are living in chaos and trauma.

Zach believes relationships change lives and every person has tremendous value to offer this world. You can hear his passion by tuning into his You Can Mentor podcast.

Zach believes God is redeeming his generational line and he desires to create a national mentoring movement in partnership with his wife, Sara, and their children Zachary Jr., Stephen, and Joanna. In his spare time, Zach enjoys listening to good music with a book in hand, discussing the intricacies of what makes a solid basketball player, or eating mass quantities of tacos.

HOW TO BREAK GENERATIONAL ~~CURSES~~ THROUGH MENTORING.

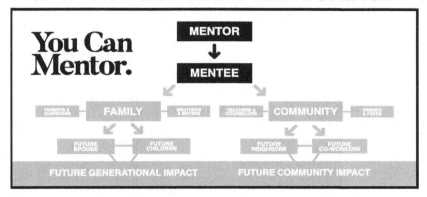

STEP ONE
Find mentors who have:

DESIRE to invest in the life of a kid from hard places.
AVAILABILITY in his schedule to effectively build a relationship.
RELATIONSHIP WITH JESUS and are active in a church.

STEP TWO
Train and support the mentor in their commitment to:

SHOW UP consistently
BUILD UP with encouragement
LOVE GOD personally

STEP THREE
The mentee will:

WATCH how their mentor lives and learn from their example
BECOME an example for others to follow.
GIVE to others what they've received from their mentor.

Nine Steps to Becoming an Ineffective Mentor:

You Can Mentor.

1
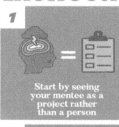
Start by seeing your mentee as a project rather than a person

2

Quickly take responsibility for their present and future success

3

Determine that your mentee needs only knowledge and resources in order to succeed

4
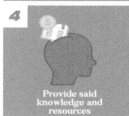
Provide said knowledge and resources

5

Watch mentee reject your help because of trust issues

6
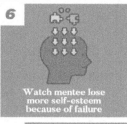
Watch mentee lose more self-esteem because of failure

7

Begin feeling your mentee is a failure and that you are as well

8

Watch mentee shut down and stop responding to you

9

Decide to quit mentoring and feel like it was all a waste of time

Nine Steps to Becoming an Effective Mentor:

You Can Mentor.

1

Start by recognizing their hurts and unrealized trauma

2

Quickly take on the responsibility to show up and love your mentee no matter what

3

Rather than be offended or discouraged, seek to understand the reasons behind their actions

4

Be a consistent presence of unconditional love

5

Build relationship, earn their trust, and speak truth to heal their sense of self

6

Pray for God to reveal to you how he sees them

7

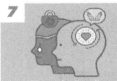

Trust the Lord's timing when things get tough and when progress is lost

8

Trust God to transform their life as you love them well

9

By God's grace, they will feel loved and empowered to fulfill their potential

You Can Mentor.

The Mentoring Resource for Christian Mentors and Mentoring Organizations

THE POTENTIAL AND
PAIN OF RELATIONSHIP

You Can Mentor.

THE POTENTIAL OF RELATIONSHIP	THE PAIN OF RELATIONSHIP
NEEDS MET *"I'm getting what I need"* - Attention - Affirmation - Acceptance	**NEEDS UNMET** *"I'm not getting what I need"* - Ignored - Rejection - Disapproval
BELIEVING TRUTH *"I'm important."* - Confidence	**BELIEVING LIES** *"I don't matter."* - Insecurity
FEELS GOOD *"I am cared for."* - Loved - Grateful - Joyful	**FEELS BAD** *"I am neglected."* - Hurt - Angry - Fear
LEADS TO RIGHT ACTIONS *"I will be considerate."* - Kindness - Generosity - Pursuing excellence	**LEADS TO WRONG ACTIONS** *"I will act out to be seen."* - Perfectionism - Manipulative - Rebellious
LEADS TO A FULFILLED LIFE *"I will provide for others."* - Healthy family - Caring relationships - Maturity - Forgiving	**LEADS TO AN UNFULFILLED LIFE** *"I can't trust anyone."* - Conflicted family - Poor character - Immaturity - Holds grudges

This resource is adapted from the **Center for Relational Care**

relationalcare.org

Citations

1. Jane Ellen Stevens, "Nearly 35 Million U.S. Children Have Experienced One or More Types of Childhood Trauma," ACEs Too High, April 25, 2017, https://acestoohigh.com/2013/05/13/nearly-35-million-u-s-children-have-experienced-one-or-more-types-of-childhood-trauma/.

2. "Understanding Child Trauma." *SAMHSA* online. Accessed March 1, 2021. https://www.samhsa.gov/child-trauma/understanding-child-trauma/.

3. "The Extent of Fatherlessness." *Fathers.com* online. Accessed March 1, 2021. https://fathers.com/statistics-and-research/the-extent-of-fatherlessness/.

4. Chris McGreal, "About 13m US Children Are Living below the Poverty Line, Rights Group Reveals," The Guardian (Guardian News and Media, April 30, 2019), https://www.theguardian.com/law/2019/apr/30/us-children-poverty-childrens-defense-fund-report.

5. "The Fatherless," Forerunner Mentoring Program, accessed March 10, 2021, https://www.forerunnermentoring.com/the-fatherless.

Made in the USA
Monee, IL
16 April 2022

94845484R00089